Essentials of Management for Healthcare Professionals

T0292877

Essentials of Management for Healthcare Professionals

By

Hari Singh

Former Director, Institute of Health Management Research,
Bangalore, India
Country Representative, EngenderHealth India
Project Director, The RESPOND Project, India
Executive Director, Foundation for Research in
Health Systems, India
Director, Clinical Services, Marie Stopes, India

CRC Press
Taylor & Francis Group
Boca Raton London New York

CRC Press is an imprint of the
Taylor & Francis Group, an **informa** business

A PRODUCTIVITY PRESS BOOK

CRC Press
Taylor & Francis Group
6000 Broken Sound Parkway NW, Suite 300
Boca Raton, FL 33487-2742

First issued in paperback 2020

© 2018 by Hari Singh
CRC Press is an imprint of Taylor & Francis Group, an Informa business

No claim to original U.S. Government works

ISBN 13: 978-0-367-73540-1 (pbk)
ISBN 13: 978-1-138-29748-7 (hbk)

Library of Congress Cataloging-in-Publication Data

Names: Singh, Hari, author.
Title: Essentials of management for healthcare professionals / Hari Singh.
Description: Boca Raton : Taylor & Francis, a CRC title, part of the Taylor & Francis imprint, a member of the Taylor & Francis Group, the academic division of T&F Informa plc, 2018. | Includes bibliographical references and index.
Identifiers: LCCN 2017037819| ISBN 9781138297487 (hardback : alk. paper) | ISBN 9781315099200 (ebook)
Subjects: LCSH: Health services administration.
Classification: LCC RA971 .S54 2018 | DDC 362.1--dc23
LC record available at https://lccn.loc.gov/2017037819

Visit the Taylor & Francis Web site at
http://www.taylorandfrancis.com

and the CRC Press Web site at
http://www.crcpress.com

Dedicated to my mother

Inderjeet Kaur

Contents

Contributors

The following colleagues made valuable contributions to this book:

- Mr. S.S. Sandhu, General Manager-Finance, Airport Authority of India (retired)
- Professor A.L. Shah, Professor, IIHMR University, Jaipur
- Dr. Pavan Gurha, MD, FICA, Head, Department of Anesthesiology and Critical Care, Batra Hospital, New Delhi, India
- Dr. Prithpal Singh Sethi, Family Physician, Delhi, India
- Dr. Rakesh Pandey, Consultant-Pediatrics, Sandwell & West Birmingham NHS Trust, London
- Dr. Rakesh Ghosh, Senior Data Scientist, UCSF Global Health Sciences, University of California, San Francisco
- Dr. Vivek Ranjan, Senior Consultant Gynecology-Obstetrics, Government Hospital, Najafgarh, Delhi, India.
- Dr. Kapil Garg, Chief Operating Officer, Paras Hospital, Gurgaon, India
- Dr. T.S. Daral, Medical Superintendent (retired), Rajiv Gandhi Super Specialty Hospital, Delhi, India
- Dr. Nandkumar Jairam, Chairman and Group Medical Director, Columbia Asia Group of Hospitals, India
- Dr. Rakesh K. Chaturvedi, Director-Medical Services, Batra Hospital and Medical Research Center, New Delhi, India
- Mr. Sameer Mehta, Director, HOSMAC, Mumbai, India

- Mr. Senthil Nathan, Director, Service Strategia, Bangalore, India
- Rupinder Kaur, Lt Col (Retired), Health Unit, American Embassy, New Delhi
- Aradhika Singh, Lecturer, Delhi School of Arts, New Delhi
- Reema Singh, Student
- Rini Singh, Student
- GC Jain, Director, CUTS International, Jaipur, India

Preface

There is a general feeling among medical professionals that their status and respect in the community is declining. It is said that earlier doctors were treated as next to God. But, now they are being looked at with suspicion. Some people feel doctors are greedy; they recommend expensive tests and treatment for their personal benefit; they trap patients in the intensive care unit to extract money. On the other hand, medical professionals are of the view that people spend lavishly on their comforts, entertainment, and luxuries, but when there is a question of paying for their medical expense, they want free treatment. There might be a reason behind this mindset. In many countries, in the past, medical services were predominantly provided by government hospitals and charity-run hospitals, which were free or subsidized. These establishments played an important role in providing medical care for people; although, there were many deficiencies in the services they provided. Hospitals were overcrowded and patients had to wait long and experience a great deal of uncertainty. Some service providers had no concern for the pain or suffering of patients; they did not care for their dignity and behaved rudely. In cases of medical negligence, it was not uncommon for authorities to connive with erring professionals. Despite all this, patients did not express any dissatisfaction, primarily because the services were free or subsidized. What is more, there was no other option for them.

This scenario has since changed. Medical care is now an industry and private providers and hospitals are the major service providers. They operate on business principles. Hospitals are becoming highly specialized and complex. Diagnostics and therapeutics are technology intensive. Private establishments have to compete with one another to remain in business. They strive to induct the best talent and latest technical know-how, resulting in ever-increasing costs to patients. Patients, who pay high charges, demand quality as a matter of right. To meet the challenge, hospitals are compelled to introduce professionalism into their systems and services. They appoint qualified professional managers to manage their clinics and hospitals with a view to allowing health professionals to focus on clinical care. Whether right or wrong, "management" is often associated with authority and power. As a result, the medical professionals are reduced to a secondary level in some organizations. To retain a commanding positions in medical organizations, it has become necessary for healthcare professionals to learn "management," at least its basics.

On the other hand, nonmedical managers, while managing healthcare services, do not get the required cooperation from medical professionals, as the latter are often secretive and unwilling to share medical knowledge. If medical knowledge is demystified, nonmedical managers can proficiently perform many functions in healthcare organizations. Both medical and nonmedical managers can complement each other in providing quality healthcare services.

This book aims to orient doctors and other healthcare professionals on the essentials of business management, and to familiarize them with management terms and jargon. They can learn to be effective managers besides being health professionals. Similarly, nonmedical managers can become familiar with the nuances of clinical care and special managerial requirements of healthcare facilities. They all will be able to relate processes in healthcare settings with the concepts of business management. They can develop expertise in patient relationship management and contribute to enhancing patient satisfaction in their facilities. This will also reduce the possibility of conflicts. Still, they can be prepared to face aggrieved and agitated clients and manage conflicts if need be. They will be equipped to develop business plans to expand their business or to start a new venture and estimate possible financial returns on investment. This book is meant for doctors, nurses, and practitioners from other systems of medicine, and non-medicos who hold a managerial position in healthcare organizations or who are considering assuming one in future. It may also be useful for practitioners who would like to manage their clinics professionally or expand their business. It is a resource book for the students and faculty of Master of Public Health (MPH), Master of Hospital Administration (MHA)/ Master of Hospital Management (MHM) and related courses. Even students of business management may find it useful.

In This Book

In this book we have uniformly used gendered pronouns: "he" or "his" for the managers, healthcare professionals, clients, and others. This is only for the convenience of writing and there is no intention of any bias against women.

When a person falls sick or is injured, his entire family is affected. In a hospital, it is not uncommon to see a patient sitting in a wheelchair in one corner of the waiting area, while his family members do the running around to get the patient registered. Therefore, we consider the family members of a patient equally important and use the term "client" instead of "patient." Clients include patients, their family members, friends, or whoever visits them when they are admitted to a hospital. It should be understood that all clients who use hospital services are not patients. For example, pregnant women visit hospitals for antenatal checkups or delivery, and children receive immunizations. Similarly, healthy adults undergo executive health checkups or avail of family planning services. These are the clients, but not the patients, of a hospital. Accordingly, in this book we have mostly used the term "clients" for patients. However, since "patient satisfaction" is a generic and popular term, it is used as such.

Every effort has been made to keep the book simple and lucid. One should be able to read it like a novel, without much effort.

Chapter 1

Introduction to Management

Management, in the context of healthcare organizations, can be defined as the science and art of guiding the human and physical resources of an organization toward satisfying the health related needs and expectations* of the clients.

A hospital manager's foremost consideration is that the clients receive appropriate treatment, and that they are fully satisfied with the services they receive. To achieve this, the manager ensures that the staff deployed is friendly, courteous, and reassuring. They do not compromise on their safety at any cost. They are technically competent to provide quality clinical services and care. A manager also ensures that the work environment in the organization is pleasant, lively, and conducive for the staff to remain in high spirits.

In the process of providing services, resources are utilized, which in a hospital setting include manpower, medicine, sterile instruments, equipment, consultation chambers,

---

* There is a subtle difference between "needs" and "expectations." A client or community has certain "expectations" from the services providers. The "needs" of a client or community are those that are felt by them or assessed by healthcare professionals. Both are important from management's perspective.

1

inpatient beds, operating rooms, computer services, electricity, and water. An important consideration for a hospital manager is to ensure that these resources are utilized effectively and efficiently. The difference between effectiveness and efficiency should be understood. Effectiveness is the degree to which desired results are achieved. In other words, out of what was expected, how much could be achieved. If in a hospital, 80 beds are occupied out of a total of 100 beds, the hospital can be considered 80% effective in utilizing its beds. Efficiency refers to achieving something with minimum resources. Efficiency is measured as a ratio of output to input. The average length of stay of patients in a hospital indicates its efficiency in utilizing its beds. With a shorter length of stay and a faster turnover of patients, more patients can be treated on the same number of beds, resulting in a higher profit and, therefore, higher efficiency. However, if many beds are vacant and there are not many new clients who might require admission, the hospital does not gain financially by reducing the length of stay of patients. Only when bed occupancy is high, will reducing the length of stay be beneficial. Thus, effectiveness is a prerequisite of efficiency. In other words, efficiency is meaningless without effectiveness.

Another important consideration for a manager is increasing the organization's profit. In this context, there are two broad possibilities. Firstly, efforts can be made to increase the utilization of services and secondly, the cost of providing the services needs to be kept under control. A hospital earns a major portion of its profit from operation rooms, laboratories, radiology, pharmacy, and intensive care units. These are known as the "profit centers" of a hospital. The number of operating rooms and intensive care beds are increasing in modern hospitals, with a view to increasing profits. It should be noted that outpatient clinics and inpatient beds do not yield considerable financial returns directly, but still they are important as they provide the clients for the profit centers. Most of the patients are admitted to wards through outpatient clinics.

Most of the patients who need major surgeries are first admitted in wards. Thus, profit centers are dependent on outpatient clinics and inpatient beds.

Ensuring the quality of services is necessary to sustain the clientele. The manager needs to ensure that the outcomes of the treatment are comparable to national or international standards. Thus, for a hospital manager, effectiveness, efficiency, and quality of services in the hospital, and client satisfaction are important concerns.

Management Levels

Many old books on management refer to three levels of management:

■ First-line managers
■ Mid-level managers
■ Top-level managers

Nowadays, organizations do not strictly follow this classification; still an understanding of these levels can be helpful to understanding the human resource matrix of an organization:

First-Line Managers

First-line managers are also known as supervisors. They supervise frontline workers or technicians. They are generally promoted from frontline workers or technicians; accordingly, they possess the expertise of frontline work. They work in close association with their subordinates, they support and coach them to work with perfection. First-line managers are responsible for timely completion of the work.

In a hospital setting, supervisors are generally posted in support service departments, such as the central sterile supply department, linen and laundry department, kitchen, medical gases and pipeline unit. There can be more than one supervisor in a department. For example, in the central sterile supply department, one supervisor oversees autoclaving, and the other supervises the distribution of sterile supplies to user departments and the collection of used items. The first supervisor ensures that all autoclaves are functional, all posted technicians are available on duty, and that they all team up to complete the process of sterilization of the materials collected from the user departments in a timely manner. The second supervisor ensures the timely distribution of the sterile supplies to each user department and the collection of used materials. Similarly, in the hospital kitchen, one supervisor supervises cooking and the other supervises the distribution of meals to the admitted patients.

In healthcare organizations, first-line managers supervise outreach workers or village-level workers. Outreach workers are generally involved in promoting awareness among people in rural and remotes areas. Some of them also provide healthcare services, such as family planning services, presumptive treatment of malaria, or providing oral rehydration solution (ORS) for diarrhea in children. The first-line managers are generally positioned at the district level or below.

Mid-Level Managers

Middle-level managers are generally in charge of a support department. They are responsible for the proper functioning of the department, as well as the quality of services or products.

In a hospital setting, a middle-level manager is generally in charge of a support service department, such as the central sterile supply department, kitchen, medical records department, hospital pharmacy, linen and laundry unit, or medical gases and pipeline unit. The manager of the central sterile supply department is responsible for the effective functioning of the department, the quality of sterile supplies and their distribution. He would supervise the first-line managers of the department. He would coordinate with other related departments, such as the linen and laundry department, operating rooms, and other user departments, and he would ensure that their requirements for sterile supplies are fulfilled.

In the context of healthcare organizations, middle-level managers are generally positioned at the state or province level. A state program manager supervises several district-level managers.

Top-Level Managers

Top-level managers are in charge of major departments. They ensure the smooth functioning of the department, its effectiveness and efficiency. They are responsible for the profitability of the center, quality of services, and patient safety. They contribute to the formulation of rules, regulations, protocols and guidelines for their departments. They may also be involved in the strategic planning of the organization. In a hospital setting, the following departments are generally headed by top-level managers:

- Clinical services
- Support services
- Human resources department
- Accounts and finance
- Marketing department

Organizational Structure of a Hospital

The head of hospital is generally known as the chief executive officer (CEO), executive director (ED), managing director (MD), or director. He supervises a number of top level managers, such as medical director, finance director, and HR director. Top level managers supervise mid-level managers; for example, the head of support services supervises those in charge of engineering services and of food and beverages services. Mid-level managers further supervise frontline supervisors; for example, the food and beverages manager supervises the pantry supervisors and kitchen supervisor. An example of the organizational structure of a typical corporate hospital is presented in Table 1.1.

Organizational Structure of an NGO

In the case of nongovernmental organization (NGOs) and international NGOs, the head of a country program is generally known as the country director. These days, terms such as CEO, ED, or MD are also used for this position. The country director is assisted by an operations director, finance manager, and human resources manager. Some organizations employ a business development manager and monitoring, learning and evaluation (MLE) manager. Organizations that provide services many have manager/assistant manager-procurement. All these positions are generally based at the national headquarters.

For implementation of the program at the province level, there may be province program managers. Province level managers may be assisted by district-level managers. The district-level managers may supervise subdistrict-level supervisors, who may further supervise village-level workers or outreach workers.

In such a structure, the national-level managers can be considered top-level managers. The province level and district-level managers are mid-level managers. Subdistrict-level personnel are frontline supervisors (Table 1.2).

Functions of Management

Managers are generally responsible for managing the day-to-day functioning of an organization or a facility, a program, or an activity. Top-level managers are often involved in preparing plans for the future or in envisioning for the organization. The three cardinal functions performed by most of the managers are

- Planning
- Implementation
- Evaluation

Table 1.1   Organizational Structure of a Large Corporate Hospital

	Chief Executive Officer (CEO)/Executive Director (ED)/Managing Director (MD)/Director (Head of Organization)					
Top-level Managers	Medical Services	Nursing Services	Support Services	Human Resources	Finance	Marketing
	Medical director/director-medical services/medical superintendent	Nursing director/director-nursing services/nursing superintendent	Non-medical administrator/head of support services	Director-human resources	Chief financial controller/chief finance officer/director-finance	Director-marketing
	Head of the departments (HODs) of clinical services, laboratory medicine, radiology	Deputy nursing superintendent	Chief engineer	Manager talent management		

(Continued)

Table 1.1 (Continued) Organizational Structure of a Large Corporate Hospital

	Chief Executive Officer (CEO)/Executive Director (ED)/Managing Director (MD)/Director (Head of Organization)					
Top-level Managers	*Medical Services*	*Nursing Services*	*Support Services*	*Human Resources*	*Finance*	*Marketing*
Mid-level Managers	Manager-medical record section, manager-HMIS, manager-quality assurance, senior medical social worker, manager-inpatient services, manager-intensive care unit	Assistant nursing superintendent, ward in-charge, infection prevention nurse, nurse educator	Manager-materials/manager-procurement/manager-stores, manager-front office, manager-CSSD, manager-housekeeping, manager-laundry and linen, manager-food and beverages/kitchen manager, civil engineer, electrical engineer, biomedical engineer	Manager-HR/personnel manager	Manager-finance/manager accounts, cashiers	Manager-marketing, public relations officer (PRO)

Note: HMIS, hospital management information system; CSSD, central sterile supply department; HR, human resources.

Table 1.2 Organizational Structure of an NGO in a Country

	Operations manager	Finance manager	Country Director (Head of Organization) Human resources manager	MLE manager	Business development manager
Top-Level Managers					
Mid-Level Managers	Province program manager	Assistant manager-accounts	Assistant manager-human resources	Assistant manager-MLE	
	District program manager	Finance officer		MLE officer/program officer	
Frontline Supervisors	Subdistrict supervisors	Data entry operator			
Frontline Worker	Village-level outreach worker				

Note: NGO, nongovernmental organization; MLE, monitoring, learning, and evaluation.

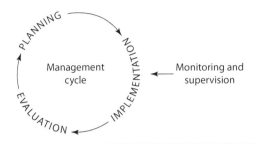

Figure 1.1   Management cycle.

First, we make a plan, and then we implement it. During the process of implementation, we monitor and supervise to check if the activities are taking place as planned. Deviations, if any, from the established plan, are identified and corrections are made. Once a task is accomplished, we evaluate to determine if we could achieve what was desired. Based on the findings, we either continue the program or revise it. The original or revised plan is again implemented and thus the cycle continues, which is known as the "management cycle" (Figure 1.1).

It should be understood that the management cycle is not only useful while setting up a new organization or starting a new program, but it is also relevant in our day-to-day life. For example, for resolving a problem, we plan some interventions, try them out, and observe carefully if they are working or not. If not, we take corrective measures or try something different. This is how the management cycle operates. The application of each function of the management cycle is explained in separate chapters.

Branches of Management

The discipline of management has evolved into many sub-specialties, such as

■ Human Resource Management
■ Organizational Behavior

- Financial Management
- Marketing Management
- Materials management or Supply Chain Management
- Operations Management
- Strategic Management

These are explained further in various chapters.

Management—Science and Art

The discipline of management entails both science and art, as explained here:

If overcrowding is an issue at the front office of a hospital, we can determine scientifically how many staff members are required at the front office to avoid clients waiting for more than five minutes in the queue. A mathematical study of waiting lines or queues is conducting through the application of queuing theory.

For obvious reasons, running out of stock out of a vital medicine can be disastrous for a hospital. On the other hand, large quantities of medicines lying in the storage occupy space, block funds, and require maintenance. There are scientific methods for determining how much quantity of a medicine should be procured at a time and at what interval would it be most cost-effective under a given consumption pattern.

Turnaround time between surgeries is an important determinant of efficiency of surgical services. It can be measured and reduced using scientific principles.

On the other hand, the discipline of management has a strong art component. Some managers maintain a lively and vibrant environment in the organization. They work in close association with staff and facilitate team building. In such teams, staff support one another and enjoy being together. Even short-tempered staff behave well. Similarly, some managers have a special expertise handling agitated clients. Not only do they calm them down, but they can convert them into loyal customers. What then is special about these managers? Well, they have mastered the art of managing people. While applications of scientific methods yield utilities in an organization, the application of art brings positivity and happiness in the working environment and they both complement each other.

Bibliography

Sharon B. Buchbinder et al., *Introduction to Health Care Management*, Jones and Bartlett Learning, 2nd edn, Burlington, MA, 2012.

Robert Emmet Burke, *Essentials of Management and Leadership in Public Health*, Jones and Bartlett Learning, Sudbury, MA, 2011.

Joan Gratto Labeler et al., *Management Principles for Health Professionals*, Jones and Bartlett Learning, 6th ed., Sudbury, MA, 2012.

Rosemary McMohan et al., *On Being in Charge*, WHO, 1992.

Lawrence F. Wolper, *Health Care Administration*, Jones and Bartlett Publishers, 5th ed., Burlington, MA, 2011.

Chapter 2

An Effective Manager

An effective manager gets the work done and produces the desired results. It is interesting to note that effective managers differ widely in their appearance, personality, temperament, interests, knowledge, and skills. They are not all extroverts; introverts make equally effective managers. Not everyone is a superior communicator. Given this, then what makes a manager effective? There is no definite answer to this question; however, a manager can improve his effectiveness by practicing the following:

Respect for Human Resources

Some managers feel their job is to keep staff members under control and make them fall in line when needed. They feel that their subordinates may take undue advantage of their leniency, so they have a need to show their authority. They consider it their prerogative to show annoyance to their subordinates or intimidate them when required. This could be because of their ignorance of management principles or distrust in them. It should be understood that there is no scope for anyone to misbehave with another person in an organization. It spoils relationships and the work environment, which is crucial for the smooth functioning of an organization. There are definite ways of dealing with poor performers without a charge of emotions, as is explained in subsequent sections.

Establishing Relationships

An effective manager opens his relationship with a subordinate with respect, trust, and confidence. The staff invariably reciprocates by making all efforts to live up to the manager's expectations. Such relationships lay the foundation of a successful organization.

Clarifying Expectations

The first concern of an effective manager is that the staff members know what is expected of them; what exactly is to be done. And then he ensures that the staff is capable of doing it and has the required means. The poor performance of staff is often not due to its inadequacies, but, because of supervisors' failure to clarify these issues. Job descriptions are generally not sufficient to explain all these. In a few positions, like that of a cashier or driver, once a staff member has understood the job, he can keep working for months or years without depending on his supervisor. But, in hospitals and healthcare organizations, most of the work is dynamic. Supervisor and supervisee must discuss what exactly the priorities are at that point of time, what needs to be done first, and what could be delayed.

Keeping Staff Motivated

Keeping the staff motivated is a big challenge in organizations. How does a manager motivate his staff? Steve Chandler, a management expert, categorically said: You cannot motivate anyone; motivation comes from within. If so, then what is it that managers do? Chandler further explained: You cannot motivate people, but you can manage an agreement with them.

Managing an Agreement with Staff

Some managers like to give instructions to each staff — what should be done and how. Peter Drucker, however, did not approve of this approach. Instructions might be necessary for the orientation of a new employee, but people who are in a job for quite some time may not like instructions. Peter Drucker suggested a better option: A manager should ask each staff, "What results should I expect of you?" Thus, the staff feels recognized. However, there can be marked differences between a manager's expectations and a staff's understanding. Raising this question itself initiates a process of communication that can help them reach an understanding at some stage. They can make an agreement to achieve certain results within a time frame. Staff members who set objectives for themselves generally work with higher commitment. Also, two-way communication enhances team spirit.

Providing Feedback

An effective manager makes it a point to provide periodic feedback to every staff member who works for him. A management expert went to the extent of saying that not providing feedback to your subordinates amounts to "cruelty." If staff members do not get regular feedback from their superiors, they tend to become either complacent or demotivated. Why do managers fail to provide timely feedback? Well, some may be ignorant of this requirement, but mostly they do not measure their subordinates' performance based on objective criteria. So, even if they are dissatisfied with someone, they are not in a position to convey it. Wherever possible, the manager should substantiate his feedback or opinion with pertinent data, evidence, or anecdotes. While providing the feedback, the manager need not be authoritative. The matter can be discussed like a routine business, without any charge of emotions. The idea is not to condemn a staff member for his poor performance, but to make him realize the situation: how the work is progressing or if there are any quality issues. This is also an opportunity to clarify doubts, if any, by either party. They may renew the agreement, if required.

Using Positive Reinforcement

Positive reinforcement is a powerful tool in shaping human behavior and performance. Recognition and appreciation of high performers is a basic requirement that must be practiced to maintain staff motivation. Exceptional performers can be rewarded, but this can be tricky as others may feel demotivated. This can be minimized by setting up a transparent system to provide equal opportunities for all to earn the reward.

Making Staff Realize the Value of Their Work

In a hospital setting, staff, such as security guards at parking lots, elevator operators, housekeeping personnel, pantry boys, laundry boys, hospital aides who move patients, cashiers, and admission desk clerks, play an important role in patient care. However, they generally do not get a sense of pride from their work. It is a manager's job to make staff members aware that the management values the work they perform, and their contribution to improving the quality of patient care. Those who take pride in their work, perform it differently. And that makes a difference in the quality of their work.

Building Productive Relationships with Staff

An effective manager not only directs his staff members to get the work done, but also facilitates enhancing their capacity to improve their performance and achieve higher-order results. He identifies subordinates' limitations and provides them with opportunities to learn new skills to overcome those limitations. On occasion, an effective manager asks his staff what support he can provide them with. Thus, a productive relationship is maintained.

The person who helps people achieve their potential is a leader, an organizational leader. An effective manager assumes a leadership role.

Utilizing the Full Potential of Staff

Staff potential is much higher than what many organizations are able to tap. How does a manager help them realize that? As discussed earlier, an effective manager expresses his full confidence and trust in his staffs. He continuously raises the bar, of course to a reasonable level, strengthens staff capacity to achieve, and gives encouragement. It is interesting to note that most employees try to live up to management's expectations.

Ability to Deal with Poor Performers

The survival of poor performers in an organization is a source of disenchantment for good performers. An effective manager understands that his staff will not respect him if he fails to discipline or get the required work done. He does not seek to be liked by everybody and he is not interested in pleasing staff by relaxing targets or standards, or by accepting poor quality work. He does not convey that everything is alright to poor performers.

Perhaps the most daunting task of a manager is to deal with poor performers. How should a manager go about this? One school of thought believes that psychotherapy of poor performers has a limited role in improving their performance. Pushing weak staff to work is not possible beyond a limit.

Insulting them does more harm than good. Managers cannot afford to waste their time and energy on such people. Then, what are a manager's options? If a manager is committed to high results, if he exhibits confidence and trust in the staff, if he makes an agreement with them and provides them with regular feedback, it will become increasingly difficult for any staff to underperform. However, if an employee does not improve after repeated feedback, the manager should not hesitate to have a straight and uncomfortable conversation with him. After making eye contact, he should communicate to him that the very reason for his existence in the organization is to get the specific work done, and if that is not done, his services are not required. A habitual poor performer will understand that his survival is going to be difficult and may leave the organization. However, the manager should be conversant with administrative procedures and well prepared to fire an employee if necessary. It is not uncommon to see poor performers surviving in some organizations because of the incompetence of their supervisors in taking administrative action.

Acquiring Knowledge of the Subject

Inadequate knowledge of the subject matter or ignorance of the realities on the ground is a major impediment to a manager's effectiveness. Many managers believe that their job is to get the work done through others, and so it is not necessary for them to know everything about the task. This is intellectual arrogance. An effective manager learns the nitty-gritty of his job, as well as that of his subordinate. For example, a manager who manages housekeeping services should know how much time and effort are required to clean a toilet in a patient's room, how much detergent or chemicals are used in this process, and what level of cleanliness should be maintained. He should know where the housekeeping staff members, after finishing their job, will keep their cleaning materials and where they can clean up, relax, and have a cup of tea. This can be learned by observing them while they are on the job and following them after. Many housekeeping managers might have never seen the entire process of cleaning a toilet. Clearly, a manager who has a thorough understanding of the work will be able to deal with staff more effectively and get better results.

While certain tasks can be learned by observing, some tasks require first-hand practical experience. A front office manager can have a better understanding of the work done by his staff by manning the front office for some time, registering a few clients, making appointments, and making financial transactions.

Peter Drucker, the well-known management expert, spoke about the unique nature or abilities of people that enhance their effectiveness. Some people write notes to memorize, regardless of whether they go over them again. Some professors revealed that sometimes they get new ideas or develop better clarity of a concept while teaching students. Some people are readers by nature while others are listeners. Readers can gather information by reading reports or glancing through hospital service statistics. Attending long meetings where people keep talking without a structured agenda or purpose may be a waste of time for them. On the other hand, a listener for whom reading long reports might be stressful, can gather crucial information quickly by interacting with key staff. Thus, one should try to identify his unique ability or style and utilize it to his advantage.

Problem-Solving Skills

An effective manager does not shy away from problems. In fact, he identifies them proactively and tries to resolve them. Staff members in organizations generally know whom to approach when they face a problem or when they are in trouble.

Situation 1

A critically sick patient reported to a hospital and the consultant advised immediate admission. The admission desk informed them of the nonavailability of a vacant bed at that moment and asked them to wait for some time. In the ward, an admitted patient was going through the discharge process and was expected to vacate his bed soon, but it took him quite some time to get the discharge summary. The critical patient got the bed after several hours of waiting. Such incidents are not uncommon in hospitals. They consume the staff's time and the patients become dissatisfied.

When confronted with a problem, a manager's first consideration is to determine whether the problem is a manifestation of a system anomaly or an isolated incident. The former is likely to recur and requires policy decisions or rules to prevent it. An isolated incident can be dealt with based on its merits. It is not uncommon to see managers firefighting recurrent problems, which could be prevented by a policy decision, rule, or guideline.

The process of problem-solving involves identifying possible options, understanding the merits and demerits of each option, and selecting one. In this case, an option for management is to make the policy decision that if a bed is not available, the staff will not ask the incoming patients to wait; they will direct them to other hospitals. Secondly, the discharge process needs to be streamlined to speed up bed turnover. Another option is to temporarily accommodate the new patient on an emergency bed, and shift him to a regular bed when available. This option, however, can interfere with emergency services and is therefore not advisable.

Management decisions should not be influenced by the staff convenience. In the context of the above example, the consultants may have reservations to providing an early discharge summary, but that should not deter management from taking an appropriate decision. Further, management should also be clear on whether an exception can be made in special circumstances; for example, if a very important person (VIP) needs admission and a bed is not available. The staff on duty should know which officer is authorized to make a decision in such situations and should have access to him.

Situation 2

In a hospital, a critically ill patient was advised to undergo a few expensive medical investigations. While awaited the medical reports, the patient died. The family members of the patient did not want to pay for the investigation and asked for a waiver. The staff concerned was persuaded, but he could not help them without the authority to waive a bill. This incident occurred during an odd hour when no senior manager was available on the premises. As a solution, the staff asked the family members to make full payment of the bill and get a refund the following day after receiving the manager's approval. We cannot expect anyone to be satisfied with such a solution.

Such a situation can recur and therefore demands a policy decision. One option is to authorize available supervisors to waive a bill up to a certain amount during odd hours and obtain ex post facto approval from the senior manager the next morning. Delegation is one of the most important yet neglected concepts in management, and it is discussed in Chapter 1, "Introduction to Management." If that is not acceptable, the supervisor ought to have the freedom to contact the senior manager at night and seek his direction. Staff should not be left to feel helpless. The manager who has the authority to make decisions should be available as close as possible to the place of action. In management terms, this concept is known as the "shortest decision pathway"

Situation 3

A patient died on the operating table in a hospital. Such an incident is rare and occurs once in several years. Although it appears to be an isolated incident, the manager has to be mindful of the fact that a problem occurring for the first time can either be an exception or the beginning of a new generic problem. Generic problems are often mistaken for isolated instances and managed on an ad hoc basis. In this example, the death could have been caused by the patient's unstable condition, equipment failure, or negligence on the service provider's part. An unstable patient's death on the operating table is an exception, whereas equipment failure or providers' negligence is likely to recur if corrective measures are not taken. They need to be addressed through a policy or rule.

Golden Rule

The management of a hospital should make it explicit to its managers and staff that whenever in doubt, they should act in the best interest of the patient. Patient safety is paramount and the quality of patient care should not be compromised at any cost.

Having a Concern for Work Environment

Some managers favor one or more staff members in the organization. They consider it their personal affair to like someone who is more loyal to them, more trustworthy, or more competent. Favoritism is dangerous and may lead to factionalism, disharmony, and unhealthy competition. An effective manager strictly follows the rule of equity. If he has any personal relationships with any of the staff members, he maintains it outside the organization without doing them any undue favors.

Some managers remain confined to their office and meet with staff during formal meetings or when something goes wrong. Sometimes when a staff member visits a manager, he behaves as if the staff member is an intruder. If the staff member explains the challenges or problems, the manager puts the blame on the staff. This is not an ideal environment for work. In such an environment, the staff will avoid meeting with the manager and avoid discussing issues with him. Effective managers make it a point to meet all key staff members every day. Whenever possible, they ensure that the staff feels uplifted after the meeting. They do not remain seated in their office expecting their subordinates to come and see them. They move around in the office and meet the staff. They also encourage staff to meet each other more often. Effective managers avoid summoning staff to their chamber; rather, they go to staff workstations to discuss issues. Of course, when privacy is needed, they may call staff to their office. On occasion, they sit with staff at their desks or cabins to discuss official matters, to help them prepare a report, or reply to messages from higher office. They may guide the staff in analyzing data, interpreting reports, or resolving challenges. Such practices are helpful in creating a lively environment in the organization, wherein staff members team up, support one another, work hard, and make all possible efforts to meet and even exceed client expectations or targets. At the same time, they enjoy getting together. Sometimes get-togethers may be organized to share experiences, conduct team-building exercises, or celebrate successes. Examples of good practices or something commendable done by a staff member is appreciated and shared with others. If a mistake committed by a staff member resulted in a serious problem, the manager discusses the same without naming the individual and sensitizes all to prevent similar incidents in future. These events can be made lively and entertaining, where people get the opportunity to open up and show their talents. Care should be taken to prevent monotony in such events.

Developing Ownership for the Organization

An effective manager has a sense of ownership for his organization and its business, which is reflected in his words and actions. If he is not convinced of the utility of an assignment given by senior management, he takes up the matter with management to understand their perspective and to convey his concerns. Once a decision is made to go ahead with an assignment, he owns the responsibility for its execution. Rather than passing on the instruction to his team that the work is to be done because the management desires it, he will tell his team categorically that he wants the work to be done.

Manager as a Leader

A common understanding of a leader is that he or she can mobilize people to take certain actions. This definition is more apt for a political leader. Certainly, the person who can mobilize people to vote in his favor becomes a leader. But, here we are concerned about an organizational leader.

The most important attribute of an organizational leader is his ability to make staff members realize their potential. A person's potential is often much higher than he realizes. The leader focuses on empowering staff. He encourages them to take up higher-order responsibilities, exhibit their talent, and achieve higher results. An empowered staff can fulfill the requirements of the organization.

In addition, a leader is futuristic. He knows that every situation changes with time. He tries to understand how the needs of people and stakeholders are evolving. He tries to identify the emerging business opportunities for the organization, which is important for the sustenance of the organization.

Bibliography

Peter Ferdinand Drucker, *The Essential Drucker*, Collins Business, 2001.

Peter Ferdinand Drucker, *Classic Drucker*, Harvard Business Review, 2006.

Elizabeth Haas Edersheim, *The Definitive Drucker*, Tata McGraw-Hill, 2007.

Joan Gratto Liebler and Charles R. McConnell, *Management Principles for Health Professionals*, Jones and Bartlett Learning, 6th edn., 2012.

Steve Chandler and Scott Richardson, *100 Ways to Motivate Others: How Great Leaders Can Produce Insane Results without Driving People Crazy*, Jaico Publishing House.

Chapter 3

Time Management

Managers are often overwhelmed by official work and find it difficult to pursue something they consider important or interesting. Hospital and healthcare managers are no different. Even if this situation is due to excess work, reducing the work load is often beyond our control. Then what can be done? How can we maintain a balance between our official work, personal interests, and family life? Well, time management is an option. How can we manage time? We cannot manage time, but we can manage ourselves to utilize time effectively. We need to prioritize our tasks and control our tendency to procrastinate. An explanation of this follows.

Prioritization

In our day-to-day life, we deal with so many issues and challenges that it is no wonder that we get lost in chores and end up doing something that is not so important. As a result, important or interesting activities get neglected. Time is limited; we cannot do everything. We should be clear about what is most important to our success or what will give us higher satisfaction. We need to concentrate on this and put in all efforts. This is possible only if we are willing to delegate, discard, or ignore less important things. And that is a big challenge because we have a natural tendency to not discard anything, even if we do not need it; even if we do not like it. "Prioritization" is the essence of time management. Prioritization is required in all aspects of life: professional work, family life, and personal interests. And it has to be done at every stage. The following steps can help us prioritize:

Planning

We often make the mistake of not devoting sufficient time to planning the course of our life. To save time, we sometimes plunge straight into action. The following story illustrates the futility of this approach. A man was once struggling to cut a tree with a blunt saw. When a passer-by asked him, "Why don't you first sharpen your saw?" He said, "I have no time; I have to cut the tree before the sun sets." He did not understand the simple fact that without sharpening the saw, he will not be able to cut the tree. Similarly, without proper planning, we are not likely to achieve anything great in life. Brian Tracy said, "If you are not working toward your own goals, you are working toward someone else's." We need to plan to take control of our lives. Sometimes we are not able to plan because we do not know what exactly we want to achieve in life, or we lose sight of a desired goal.

Goal Setting

We should be clear of what exactly we want to achieve in life or in our vocation. In other words, we must have a goal. We can also have multiple goals related to our official work, personal interests, or family life. These can be long term or short term.

Reviewing

Every day we should ask ourselves: Am I moving toward my goal? Whatever I did yesterday, will it be helpful in taking me toward my goal? Before accepting a major activity, we should ask the same question.

A daily calendar can be helpful in planning. It can be managed conveniently on a mobile phone or computer. We may start our day by reviewing the calendar. After going through pending tasks from the previous day, we can note down the activities that we would like to take up during the day, and draw a plan to execute them systematically. In the evening, we should review what was accomplished and what remained incomplete or unattended. Reasons for any shortfall can be examined. If necessary, pending tasks can be reentered into the next day's schedule. Anything that stays in the calendar for longer than a month without any action may be dropped.

Overcoming Crisis

No matter how meticulously we plan, we come across crisis situations in our life, and we have to put aside our plans to deal with them. After a crisis is over, ironically, we get lost in chores and fail to revert to our original plan. And that is the tragedy. Consequently, we forget our goal for days, months, or sometimes for years. And that changes the course of our life. After encountering several such failures in executing a plan, we eventually lose trust in the concept of "planning" and let life drift on its own, and that is a catastrophe. When we spend our time on meaningless activities, we feel frustrated. If we regularly remind ourselves of our goals, if we prioritize our actions at every stage and ignore less important activities, then, the possibilities of success increase.

Managing Procrastination

Procrastination is a person's inability to initiate action on a desired activity or a tendency to keep putting it off. We all procrastinate at times and keep swinging between the two extremes of action and procrastination like a pendulum. This is known as the "Action–Procrastination Continuum":

Action – Limited Action – Procrastination

There are fundamental differences in the nature of people and their basic position in the continuum. The majority of people remain between "limited action" and "procrastination," while some people are able to drive themselves toward "action." Why do we procrastinate? Common reasons are

■ We are unable to visualize potential gains from an accomplished task.
■ We do not know where to start.
■ We find the task too large to complete.
■ We have a fear of failure.
■ We dislike the task.

If we dislike a task, our inaction is quite understandable. But, if that is not the reason, our inaction demands scrutiny. Certain wrong notions promote procrastination, and we should be aware of them. For example, we postpone an activity for the next day as if there will be more time then. Similarly, if an activity is likely to take more time than we have, we happily defer it. Sometimes, we avoid an activity if we are not confident of doing it perfectly, not realizing the fact that working imperfectly is always better than putting off a task indefinitely.

The following techniques can help us in overcoming procrastination:

Start Immediately

Many people have great ideas. The key to success is not in having great ideas, but in being able to execute them. Not getting started is a major barrier. The more times we postpone a desired action, increasingly, it becomes difficult to start. Therefore, it is important that once we make a decision to do something, we must take the first step immediately to overcome inertia. This is perhaps the most effective way of preventing procrastination. The rule of two minutes is that any desired action that comes to mind all of a sudden and that can be accomplished in two minutes, must be taken up immediately, leaving everything aside.

Break the Task into Smaller Pieces

If the task is big and cannot be completed in one go, it can be sliced into small pieces, but the first part must be taken up immediately. We can schedule a slot every day for completing the remaining parts and set a deadline. There is a general tendency to allocate less time, and if the task is not accomplished, we feel frustrated. Therefore, allocating a realistic amount of time is important.

If we are able to successfully initiate a task and complete a part of it or the entire task, we can reward ourselves. This is motivating.

Start with the Hardest Part

We overcome a hidden fear by attempting the hardest part first. It can change our perception and the rest of the task may become easier. However, in examinations, it is advised to complete the easy questions first. It should be understood that the two situations are quite different. In an examination, we have the short-term objective of securing maximum marks; whereas, in life, we have long-term aims.

Batch Similar Activities

When we work on an activity, our mind gets tuned to it and it becomes easier for us to do similar things. For example, when we write an email, writing a few more emails may not be difficult. By scheduling an activity at the same time every day, we take advantage of the habit. We can fix time slots for all our major activities, such as replying to emails, conducting review meetings, or meeting visitors.

Visitors dropping into a manager's office on and off can be highly disruptive, and if they know that the manager meets the visitors during a fixed time only, they start following the rule. We are programmed to drop everything to answer a telephone call. Unnecessary telephone calls interrupt important activities and break the continuity of our thoughts and actions; they waste our time. To avoid such interruptions, we can devote a set time every day to make telephone calls. In some cases, we can even ask callers to contact us during that time.

Share the Commitment

People generally perform better when they know someone is watching them. Our commitment increases if we inform our professional colleagues, friends, and family members of what we are trying to achieve.

Develop Habits

While learning to drive a car, we have to think before taking an action. For example, on encountering an obstacle, we first think of applying the brakes and then we actually apply them. After some practice, we no longer think about it; such actions start happening automatically. Our mind has two parts, the conscious and the subconscious. We can control our conscious mind, but not the subconscious. In the initial stages of learning, our conscious mind controls our actions. After they have been learned, their "program" is transferred to the subconscious mind, and then the actions start happening automatically. Over time, they become a habit.

Similarly, we can develop the habit of remaining more active in the action–procrastination continuum. If we push ourselves to remain "active" for some time, it may eventually become a habit. That means that our subconscious mind takes over this function and we no longer have to strive. The time required to develop a habit varies from a few months to several years, depending on the duration of the old habit and the individual's commitment and circumstances.

Change Self-Perception

Perceiving oneself negatively as an ineffective person, a weak personality, or a poor time manager is a strong obstacle to one's achievements and growth. This negativism must be overcome by developing positive perceptions; such as, "I am determined to achieve success" or "I manage my time well." We should visualize ourselves in the new role and burn this image in our mind. Even if we pretend for some time, eventually it will become a habit and we will no longer have to act.

Sometimes we are not very comfortable doing a task; nonetheless, we are required to do it. In that case we can try to change our perception of the task by accepting it as a challenge, and playing it like a game. That is to say, not getting involved emotionally and not worrying about the results.

Specific Situations

Health and hospital managers spend most of their official time working on the computer, attending meetings, preparing documents, making supervisory rounds of departments or program areas, and meeting with visitors. In the following sections, we discuss how we can improve our efficiency in some of these functions.

Working on the Computer

Many managers receive a large number of emails every day and replying to them is time consuming. Sometimes they spend the whole day at it. We may allocate a specific slot of the day for attending to emails. After the slot is over, we may switch over to another activity. Sometimes we go through the messages hurriedly to get a sense of everything that is in the inbox. We do this with the intent of getting back to each message again to prepare a reply. This duplicates our efforts. It is suggested that while going through a message for the first time, we should decide to either reply, ignore, or delete. If we decide to reply, we should type it then and there and send it. It can be a brief reply. A prompt response, even if not very well structured, is generally better than a delayed perfect reply. Only in exceptional cases, where a significant amount of work is required to reply to an email, should we include it as a task in our calendar and execute it based on priority or schedule.

We should avoid replying to an email while being angry; in this case, we may delay the reply.

Managing Meetings

Meetings are a big time-waster in many organizations. In these meetings, one participant's talk may be of little interest to others. In many situations, a better option would be to have the concerned people meet with each other, discuss, and sort out the matter. Meetings should be called for a specific purpose, to convey management's decisions or concerns, to make a collective decision, or to seek staff opinion. Here are a few tips for conducting meetings effectively:

■ There should be a specific agenda for every meeting, which should be circulated in advance to all the participants so that they are prepared by keeping the required information ready.
■ Only the staff that are required to participate in discussions should be asked to join the meeting.
■ The meeting should start on time.
■ During meetings, the chair has an important responsibility to keep the discussions focused and bring them back to the agenda if they deviate.
■ The chair should be careful not to dominate the discussions and provide a fair opportunity to every participant to express his opinion.
■ For agreed action points, the responsible person and the deadlines should be determined.
■ Generally, a starting time is set for a meeting but not the closing time. As a result, meetings keep dragging. It is important to conclude the meetings at a set time to allow the next activity to begin.
■ The minutes of the meeting should be very brief, mainly enumerating the action points and the person responsible for those actions. The minutes should be circulated to all concerned at the earliest, preferably on the same day. Delay often defeats the purpose.
■ The next meeting should start with an update on compliance of the agreed action points of the previous meeting.

Managing Paperwork

In many organizations, managers spend a significant amount of time on paperwork that sometimes does not serve any purpose.

Example 1: A senior manager in a large hospital was in charge of the procurement section. Every day, the procurement officer submitted a large number of vouchers of routine purchases of medicines and other materials for the manager's signature. The manager was expected to sign every voucher that was put up to him without knowing whether they were genuine or not. He decided to delegate. After taking top management into confidence, he mentored the procurement officer on compliance with purchase procedures and the proper documentation. When he found the procurement officer capable of shouldering the responsibility of purchases, he delegated these to him. Under the new system, the procurement officer signed all purchase vouchers. Additionally, he prepared a summary of daily transactions and submitted it to the manager for his information. In turn, the manager took up a higher order of responsibility and spent his time more productively.

Supervisory Rounds

An important function of health and hospital managers is to make supervisory rounds of various departments of the hospital or program areas. Some managers are not very clear on their role during these rounds, and they indulge in identifying issues and faults and pointing them out to the staff concerned. By setting up effective systems, many repetitive supervisory actions can be avoided. Monitoring and supervision are explained in Chapter 11, this volume.

Dealing with Visitors

As indicated earlier, a manager should meet visitors during a fixed time slot. It may appear rude, but a manager need not offer a seat to a visitor who drops in at an odd time or without a prior appointment. If the manager feels that the visitor has important business to discuss, he can schedule a meeting later at his convenience. Or he can direct the visitor to someone else, say his assistant, for help. If there are professional chatterers who disturb the manager frequently, he can keep some problems or assignments ready to engage them in.

Socializing can help in building relations and networking, but it can also reduce our productivity. A manager can maintain a balance by keeping a slot open once a week or month for this purpose.

Saying "No"

In some cultures, it is considered rude to say "no." Even if the other person's demands are unjustified and we are not in a position to oblige. Some of us find it difficult to say "no." As a result, we go through an unpleasant process of internal conflict and waste our time. It should be understood that there is no harm in saying "no."

Chapter 4

Conflict Management

In hospitals, conflicts between patients or their family members and service providers are not uncommon. In addition, conflicts between staff members occur as in any other workplace. Most of these conflicts can be prevented or resolved. In this chapter, we will take up a few situations that commonly result in conflicts and discuss ways of resolving and preventing them.

Conflict between Client and Service Providers

Situation 1

In the emergency room of a busy hospital, the nurses and resident doctors are often overworked; they have long shifts without breaks. Since they deal with life and death, making mistakes is not acceptable. Patients with shattered body parts, amputations, or massive bleeding are a common sight for them. Sometimes many emergencies come up at the same time causing panic and chaos. Working in such an environment, day after day, causes many service providers to become immune to the pain and suffering of others. After having managed many complicated cases, sometimes service providers become less concerned about a relatively simple case. Sometimes they ask the family members of a patient to register first, before they attend to the patient. Or, they ask the patient to wait while they continue to gossip and laugh among themselves. Such behavior will not be acceptable to the family members of a patient; this can lead to an argument and conflict.

Solution: A simple way to avoid conflicts in such situations is to make sure that the service providers attend to the patient immediately and initiate the treatment. It is important for service providers to show their concern to the patient and their family members. A simple sentence, assuring them that they will receive the best possible care, can go a long way in gaining their trust. If service providers are busy attending to other emergencies, they should communicate this to the new patient or their family members, and inform them when they will be able to provide the services.

Situation 2

Sometimes patients at an advanced or terminal stage of illness, with very little chance of recovery, are admitted to an intensive care unit. They are kept alive on machines. Their family members keep making large payments to the hospital in the hope that the patient will eventually recover. They do not know that the ailment is not curable and that treatment is only going to prolong the patient's life by a couple of weeks, or months at the most. Since, the family members of such patients remain in the hospital for long periods of time, some of them may notice negligence, if any, by the service providers. For instance, if a patient develops bedsores, it is invariably due to negligence by the service providers. In one situation, the family members of a patient were told that the patient's condition was deteriorating, therefore, an MRI test was needed urgently. The family members readily agreed but nobody seemed to be in a hurry to perform the investigation; the family members had to remind the staff repeatedly to get it done. Similarly, in another situation, after conducting special tests on a patient, the results were not collected. When family members made enquiries, the attend-ing residents were clueless about the tests and their results. Under such circumstances, should a patient die, it is quite possible that his family members may accuse the hospital of negligence and refuse to pay the bill, and that may result in conflict.

Solution: Conflict in such a situation can be avoided by regularly updating family members on the patient's condition, plans for further treatment, projected expenses, and possi-bilities for recovery. It is important that service providers do not give any false hope. If a patient is likely to die, it is the responsibility of medical professionals to prepare his family members for this. It is also advisable that the family members of a critical patient be persuaded to make advance payments if he is not insured.

Situation 3

In some communities, when a patient is admitted to a hospital, many of his family members and friends visit him. If they are not allowed to see the patient, they do not hesitate to quarrel with the security guards. The hospital cannot allow too many visitors for fear of infections, and to prevent overcrowding.

Solution: Many hospitals provide one or two visitor passes per patient. Visitors can exchange the passes among them-selves, and meet the patient in turns. Some hospitals allow mobile patients to come out to a common room during visiting hours where they can meet with their visitors. Some hospitals make arrangement to accept flowers or other gifts from the visitors and pass them on to the patient through hospital staff. A nice gesture on the part of a hospital would be to arrange for a consultant, senior resident, or a nurse to come to the visitors' lobby and brief the family members in private about the condition of the patient.

Reasons for Conflicts in Hospitals

In a hospital, conflicts mostly occur when

- The needs of a patient or his family members are not fulfilled.
- Some of the service providers behave inappropriately with them.
- Required information is not provided to them.

How to Resolve Conflicts

Every conflict is unique, so there cannot be a standard formula for resolving them, but the following tips can help resolve conflicts in many situations:

- Controlling reaction
- Improving communication
- Focusing on the issue
- Dissociating people from the problem
- Fulfilling needs

Controlling Reactions

Situation 4

In the emergency room of a hospital, a patient is complaining to the staff that he has been waiting for too long and that nobody seems to be interested in attending to him. Habitual complainers tend to be angry perfectionists; they are dramatic

in their tone and gesture, and they often accuse the care providers of indifference.

Solution: It may be tempting for service providers to
respond by getting angry. They may argue that he is interfer-
ing in the treatment of other patients. But such a response is
likely to aggravate the situation. Maintaining composure can
help resolve the problem. Silence encourages the conflicting
party to gain self-control; it is difficult for a person to continue
getting angry at someone who is calm. The best solution in
such a situation would be to attend to the patient as soon as
possible without arguing or making any comments. If it is not
possible to attend to him immediately, because there are other
patients waiting, he should be informed of this and assured he
will be attended to soon.

Improving Communication

We can improve the effectiveness of our communication by
taking care of the following aspects:

- Making eye contact
- Active listening
- Providing feedback
- Using soft skills

Eye Contact

"To make oneself understood to people, one must first speak
with their eyes," said Napoleon. Not making eye contact with
the other person conveys that we are not interested. While
maintaining eye contact during a conflict, conveys our interest in resolving the issue, and the other person is likely to
follow suit. Eye contact also helps to reach a more conclusive
discussion.

Active Listening

We generally do not listen to others when we presume that we understand the issue. But that may not always be correct. A careful listener tries to understand the other person's perspective. In this process, the listener suspends his own thoughts. This type of nonjudgmental and concerned listening allows the opponent to open up, and that helps in resolving the conflict.

Providing Feedback

We cannot change others. However, we can listen to their concerns, try to understand their perspective, and provide them with honest feedback, explaining how we perceive their reaction or how we feel. Appropriate feedback encourages conflicting parties to further clarify their concern or change their behavior. While giving feedback, personal attacks and generalizations should be avoided, such as

- You always argue.
- You are only interested in fighting.
- You don't want to clear your bill that's why you are creating this entire problem.

The feedback should be neutral and without criticism and the statement should preferably be drafted in the first person, such as

- I feel frustrated when somebody blames me while I am trying my best to attend to them at the earliest.
- I don't understand why people can't wait for their turn.
- I feel bad when people do not follow the procedure.

While proper feedback can help to resolve conflict, impulsive feedback can aggravate it. Also, it should be understood that in the heat of the moment, when emotions are high, people may not accept any feedback. In such a situation, one should wait for the other person to calm down.

Using Soft Skills

Oral communication between two persons comprises three major components:

1. Spoken words
2. Tone of the voice
3. Body language

Albert Mehrabian, a communications expert, made a revolutionary discovery that words play a small role in verbal communication, whereas tone of voice, expressions, and body language have a major influence. This is contrary to common belief. Therefore, while communicating with people or trying to influence them, we should be particularly careful in keeping the tone of our voice under control and managing our body language.

Focusing on the Issue

During a conflict, it is not uncommon for people to deviate from the main issue and talk about their other grievances. In such a situation, we can assure them that those issues can be dealt with at a later stage, and encourage them to focus on the issue that led to the problem. Sometimes a difficult situation can be brought under control by reminding the conflicting parties of the key issue.

Dissociating People from the Problem

We tend to believe that problems are caused by people. Accordingly, in a conflict situation, we try to identify the person who might be responsible for it; but this does not serve any purpose. We need to keep people separate from the problem. It should be understood that people generally do not want conflict; they are just trying to fulfill their needs. However, in a stressful environment, sometimes they communicate unskillfully, leading to conflict. Being aware of this fact, we can be a little more considerate with them, and that can help resolve a conflict.

Fulfilling Needs

The most effective way of resolving a conflict is to provide the complainant with what he wants or deserves. In this context, the most important requirement is to keep one's ego under control, which is often the most challenging part of this game.

Managing Special Situations

A hospital manager should also be prepared to face exceptional situations.

Situation 5

An angry family member of a patient is standing in front of a nurse station and shouting at the nurses over some issue. How should a manager respond?

Solution: The manager should approach the person, stand in front of him, gain his attention, establish eye contact, and firmly say: "I would like to talk to you about this, please come with me," and begin to walk toward a more private space. The complainant is likely to follow. This movement itself begins to defuse tension. While walking, the manager may ask him about the issue. As mentioned earlier, the manager should try to understand his needs and try to fulfill them to the extent possible. If something is not possible, the reason should be explained.

Situation 6

A patient died while in hospital and his family members were unable to accept the situation. They called their acquaintances and a crowd gathered in the hospital. On someone's provocation, the crowd became aggressive and started damaging hospital property or even manhandling hospital staff. Although this is an exceptional situation, hospital managers should be prepared to face it.

Solution: Trying to pacify an aggressive crowd can be counterproductive. In such a situation, it is suggested that the staff should concentrate on the care of other patients. However, if the situation seems to be dangerous, staff should not hesitate to flee. Doctors wearing a white coat, if possible, should take it off and quietly become a part of the crowd and gradually disappear. Mostly, such aggressive crowds disperse soon. The staff can then return and resume work.

Conflict between Staff Members

Conflicts are inevitable when people work together in an organization, or when they are dependent on one another. Although the term "conflict" has a negative connotation, it is not always harmful. In fact, sometimes conflicts are useful if resolved amicably to the satisfaction of both parties. Potential benefits of a conflict include

■ *Improved solutions*: A conflict provides an opportunity for the management of an organization to take a deeper look into the problem. They can consider revising their policies, protocols, or guidelines to strengthen the systems and to prevent similar situations.

■ *Enhanced morale of the staff:* When staff members are involved in resolving conflicts amicably, they feel respected; their sense of belonging within the organization increases, and this raises their morale.

Organizations, where conflicts do not occur are not necessarily better off. An autocratic leadership does not allow dissent; staffs members are not allowed to question norms, practices, or decisions. Staff members that are incompetent or have no sense of belonging to an organization generally have no problem accepting anything imposed on them by management or a senior. Under such circumstances, the possibilities of conflict are reduced.

When Should a Manager Intervene?

In case there is a conflict between staff members, when should a manager intervene? It is suggested that the manager should avoid getting involved in the minor conflicts of staff members and encourage them to sort out their differences among themselves. But he should remain vigilant of what is happening. He must intervene when he finds

■ Patient care is becoming affected by the conflict
■ Staff members who were initially not involved begin to get involved
■ The discipline of the organization is at a stake

If a manager decides to intervene in a conflict between two staff members, he should meet each one of them individually and try to understand their perspective: What caused the problem, what their needs are, and what they expect from the other party? Also, according to them, what the needs of the other party are, and whether they can consider fulfilling them? After meeting them individually, the manager should call them together and ask them one by one what contribution they can make to resolve the conflict. People generally like to show that they are interested in resolving a conflict. Many conflicts can be resolved through such discussions. It may require more than one sitting, as the process of problem-solving sometimes requires peeling away the layers one by one to get to the core. It is advisable to avoid holding such meetings in the manager's office, where the manager has higher authority. The meeting should preferably be held in a neutral place like a meeting room.

If there is significant difference between the conflicting parties and they are not willing to compromise, and their differences do not affect patient care, then they may be advised to "agree to disagree" or live with their differences without fighting. On the other hand, if the manager finds that the conflict is affecting patient care and the disputants are refusing to reconcile, the manager may have to use his authority to stop them from fighting. The manager may gather information from other staff members who are not involved in the conflict, to reach a decision. He may enforce his decision on the conflicting parties. It is possible that intervening in such a manner might lead to passive resistance and manipulation by the dissatisfied party. The manager should, therefore, use his authority as a last resort.

Long-Term Measures to Prevent Conflicts

Conflicts generally occur not because of the people, but because of weak systems in organizations. The chances of conflicts increase if hierarchy in the organization is not well-defined; if the job responsibilities of staff members are not delineated or and if guidelines or protocols are not formulated. Strengthening systems by framing and implementing appropriate rules, regulations, protocols, and guidelines reduces the possibilities of conflict. System strengthening should be an ongoing process. In addition, good interpersonal communication within an organization plays a crucial role. Managers, who stay in their offices most of the time, create an environment of distrust and apprehension. They should move around in the organization, interact with staff, understand their problems and facilitate solving them before they multiply. Respecting the dignity of staff members; providing them with necessary information, and involving them in decision-making contribute to increasing a staff's sense of belonging in the organization. This contributes to creating a positive environment in the organization, which reduces the possibilities of conflict.

Bibliography

Mayor Salluzzo and Kidd Strauss. *Emergency Department Management: Principles and Applications*, Mosby, 1st edn., 1997.

Chapter 5

Legal Safety

Instances of violence against healthcare service providers and litigation against doctors and hospitals have been increasing over the years. The trust between healthcare providers and community members seems to be waning, and there are reasons for this situation. Earlier healthcare providers were highly regarded in their communities; the relationship between the two was that of provider and recipient. It was believed that financial considerations were not the sole reason for the healthcare provider to provide services to people; there were some social considerations, and many doctors worked with a motivation to help people. Accordingly, healthcare service providers enjoyed a special status and privilege in the community. Now healthcare is an industry and the medical profession is being increasingly commercialized. In a business scenario, the seller and buyer operate on an equal platform. Previous equations are no longer valid, but healthcare providers, particularly doctors, are not willing to accept the changed scenario.

Staff Behavior

As discussed in Chapter 7, "Patient Satisfaction," clients on their arrival to a healthcare facility expect someone to attend to them promptly. If a service is not possible immediately, they should be informed of the reason. They should be told when they will receive the required service.

It is important for the staff to behave in a friendly manner while dealing with clients. Client dissatisfaction or conflicts mostly occur when staff members, at some stage, behave rudely or are inattentive to clients' needs. It may be toward a security guard in the parking lot, an elevator operator, or a billing clerk. Some staff members have strong egos, they tend to take things personally and lash out at clients whose demands they perceive as irrational. Many problems in healthcare organizations can be avoided if all staff members behave nicely with the clients. A client may ignore many shortcomings in the delivery of services if staff behavior is good. Staff needs to be reminded periodically of the fact that clients are the most important stakeholders in the organization; all possible efforts need to be made to meet their requirements. It is also important to make staff members realize that they will be confronted with clients who may not behave well or who may have irrational demands. Nonetheless, staff should try to resolve their concerns in a polite manner. However, if something is not manageable, the staff member should immediately contact a supervisor rather than trying to sort out everything by himself. Role play is a very effective pedagogy to train staff to manage difficult people.

Communication with Clients

The clients expect healthcare providers to express concern for their pain or suffering. Healthcare providers are required to explains to clients the nature of their problem, the proposed course of treatment, and the possible outcomes. This is to be done while being cautious not to offer any false assurances.

If the condition of a client deteriorates, this must be conveyed to the client and his family members. Documentation that the client's family members were informed of the deteriorating condition can be helpful in managing litigation. Similarly, if a client is likely to die, it must be communicated, and it would be prudent to ask them to write down that they have been informed of and have understood the possible adverse outcomes. Communicating effectively with clients is the key to establishing a relationship with them, increasing their satisfaction, and reducing the possibilities of conflict and litigation.

Justify Actions

Sometimes healthcare providers, out of their concern for the clients, their economic status, or some social obligations agree to compromise with the standard clinical protocols. For example—a poor client is suffering from fever, the provider wants to rule out malaria, dengue, and typhoid but on consideration of economic condition of the client, he can put the client on symptomatic treatment for three days and then if required, go for the investigation. It would be prudent for the provider to write on the client's record that investigations are needed to rule out the previously mentioned conditions; however, keeping in view the economic and social constraints of the client, medicines are being tried for three days and thereafter position would be reviewed.

Documentation

Client records are legal documents and they play an important role in safeguarding healthcare providers.

Example: An obese client was operated on for intestinal obstruction. Postoperatively, she was recommended complete bed rest. Many of her family members or relatives would visit her and stay with her for quite some time. The attending resident doctor objected to visits by so many people, but they refused to listen to him. The resident doctor wrote in the client records that despite repeated advice, a large number of visitors met the client and posed a risk of infection for her. Every time he noticed the unwanted visitors, he made a note of it. A few days after the surgery, the client was allowed to start a liquid diet. However, during his rounds, the resident found the client eating solid and spicy food brought in by her visitors from outside. The resident objected to it and wrote in the client records that the client was found eating solid and spicy food against medical advice. After a few days, the client developed an infection at the surgical site leading to a "burst abdomen." She was operated on again, but a few days after the second surgery, she died. The client's party filed a case of negligence in the consumer court, but the case was summarily rejected because of the meticulous client records kept by the senior resident.

If a large number of people accompany a client in an emergency and some of them show aggression or misbehave with a service provider, it is advisable to make a note of it in the client records.

Not only should negative experiences be recorded, every important activity that contributes to the treatment, such as when suction is performed or nebulization is provided, should be recorded.

Obtaining Consent

Before any surgery or risky procedure consent is, generally, obtained from the client in the presence of a witness. Consent should be informed, meaning that the client should have gone through the entire consent form, or somebody should read it to the client and then the client signs the agreement. Family members of a client can sign the consent form only if the client is not an adult or is not in a mental or physical condition to sign. Obtaining blind consent for any procedure, under any type of anesthesia, may have no legal sanctity. Therefore, consent should be obtained for a specific procedure only. If anesthesia will be required, the type of anesthesia should be specified.

Besides this, there are many situations in which service providers can be relieved of responsibilities by getting client consent. For example: A client needs to be moved to a different center but the client family does not want to move the client elsewhere; they insists on continuing the treatment where the client is. This should be documented. Preferably, the client or his family members should write, in their own handwriting, that they want to keep the client in that facility even though the doctor has advised a referral. If a client needs surgery or a procedure but the client family does not want to follow the advice, they should be asked to write down that they are not willing to submit to the surgery advised by the surgeon. Documentation can play an important role in safeguarding the interests of healthcare service providers in litigation.

Timely Referral

It is obligatory for healthcare providers to attend to an emergency. If the level of expertise is not optimal for managing a particular client, the client should be stabilized and referred as soon as possible. The referral slip should indicate the condition of the client at the time the client was received, the treatment provided, and the reason for referral. It is important to mention the time at every stage, particularly in the case of emergency clients. If there is any delay in getting an equipped ambulance to move the client, this should be recorded in the client records as well. If the client is not moved because of the risk involved in moving him, it should be documented.

Indemnity Scheme

It is important for doctors and hospitals to be indemnified, so that compensation awarded to a client is paid by an insurance company and not by the service provider, in the case of successful litigation by the client's party.

Membership of Professional Bodies

It is useful to be a member of relevant professional bodies and maintain a cordial relationship with one's peers. They can be of assistance in a time of need.

Security Arrangements

Setting up closed circuit television cameras in important locations and employing the services of trained security guards can be helpful. Mock drills are very useful in training and preparing security personnel to deal with difficult situations.

Community-Based Healthcare Programs

In community-based healthcare programs, if the healthcare workers are required to work in a new area, move house-to-house, and interact with community members, it is advisable to take certain precautions.

Example: A team of investigators for a national family health survey was collecting household data in a rural area. The questionnaire included information on the income of a family and its assets, such as televisions, motor bikes, and so on. There were some thefts in the area while the data collection was in progress. A rumor spread that the investigators were the agents of the thieves and were collecting information about people's assets.

During such exercises, the team should have a proper letter of authority indicating what the executing organization is, program information, and what exactly they are required to do. Team leaders should meet the officials concerned in the region, such as district collector or chief medical or health officer, and take them into confidence, and try to obtain a letter from them that allows them to carry out the project activities. They can try to get a letter, addressed to the facility in charge of peripheral institutions, asking for their cooperation and support in carrying out program activities.

There are leaders or opinion leaders in each community, such as elected representatives or individuals respected by the community, say a teacher or postmaster, or a healthcare worker. It is useful to first contact such people, take them into confidence, and seek their consent before venturing out to the streets or households.

In unknown places, particularly rural or tribal areas, healthcare workers should be dressed decently, keeping in mind the local traditions. They must not consume alcohol or other intoxicants and must maintain dignity in their behavior. Supervisors should brief team members on such issues before they venture out for community-based activities. They should remain vigilant observing staff activities during such endeavors.

Chapter 6

Quality Improvement

Clinical services are like a double-edged sword. While quality clinical services contribute to improving the health, well-being, and longevity of people, poor quality services can be harmful and even dangerous. Measuring the quality of clinical care has been challenging since the natural progress of a disease varies among individuals. Different people react differently to the stress of an illness. Their physiological response to the same treatment also varies. Despite these constraints, healthcare organizations have made impressive progress in measuring the quality of clinical care and improving it.

Historical Background

Florence Nightingale, while treating Crimean War victims in the 1860s, realized the importance of quality patient care. She collected data systematically, and found that mortality rates were higher in larger hospitals with overcrowded wards. She also determined that patients who stayed in hospital longer had higher chances of dying. Through a controlled trial, she demonstrated how the mortality rate in a hospital can be sig-nificantly reduced by improving sanitary conditions; that is, by providing clean bed sheets, clean drinking water, and food to patients, along with dressing their wounds using clean bandages. These were revolutionary findings that allowed authorities to realize the importance of hygiene and sanitation. The significance of research and the use of biostatistics in decision-making was also learned during this time.

In 1910, in the United States, Dr. Abraham Flexner highlighted the poor quality of medical education. The government consequently shut down 60 medical schools out of a total of 155. In 1913, the American College of Surgeons was established, and one of its explicit goals was to improve the quality of patient care in hospitals. Dr. Ernest A. Codman was the first to assess the quality of care and studied its end results in 1914. He emphasized the importance of accreditation of institutions and certification of service providers in assuring quality.

Encouraged by the success of the American College of Surgeons, in 1952, the Joint Commission on Accreditation of Hospitals/Healthcare Organizations (JCAHO) was established in the United States. The commission aimed at encouraging voluntary attainment of high standards of institutional care by healthcare organizations. The international wing of the organization is known as the Joint Commission International (JCI) and provides accreditation to hospitals outside the United States.

With the growing concern for consumer protection and human rights in the United States, during the 1960s, a hospital was held responsible for the negligence of a doctor in a legal suit. This was the first time a hospital was held accountable for medical negligence on the premise of a hospital having the authority to regulate the clinician's practice. The quality of patient care thus became an institutional affair. Now a days, hospitals are penalized for negligence or malpractice by their doctors.

Management experts from industry, such as Walter Andrew Shewhart, W. Edwards Deming, Joseph Juran, and Kaoru Ishikawa played important roles in advancing the concept of quality, its approaches, and techniques. Terms like quality assurance (QA), quality improvement (QI), total quality management (TQM), and continuous quality improvement (CQI) were coined at different points in time and each term emphasized specific aspects of quality.

TQM emphasizes the need to involve all the departments and personnel of an organization in improving the quality of services. It also emphasizes improving structure and processes for better output. In a hospital, everything matters as far as quality is concerned, from the parking facilities, the registration process, and the arrangements to move a patient, to the actual clinical care.

CQI emphasizes that there is no limit to improving quality. Quality improvement is a continuous, ongoing, and infinite process.

These days, many fancy terms are attached to quality. Bill Smith, an engineer at the Motorola Company, in 1986, introduced the concept of "six sigma" for quality improvement. It was later adopted by General Electric. These companies and many others that adopted this concept became very successful, and accordingly, the term six sigma became popular. Six sigma is a statistical model that denotes 3.4 or less defects per million activities. That means achieving perfection, to almost zero defect. The concept emphasizes focus on client expectations, systems and processes, and data-driven decision-making. The steps for quality improvement are: Define, measure, assess, improve, and control (DMAIC). Some practitioners claim to combine lean processes with six sigma and call it "lean six sigma," and some practitioners have coined terms such as lean six sigma black belt. In the health sector, however, generic terms like "quality improvement" or "quality assurance" are commonly used for quality improvement interventions.

Determinants of Quality

The quality of clinical care can be measured through the following factors:

1. Effectiveness of clinical care
2. Safety
3. Patient satisfaction

Effectiveness of the Clinical Care

People generally avail of clinical care to alleviate their pain and suffering, cure diseases, heal injuries, restore functionality of organs and limbs, or to save a life. Clinical care can be considered effective if it fulfills the requirements of a client. In other words, clinical care is effective if it improves the condition of patients, provides them with some relief, or cures them. Their effectiveness is dependent on the clinical competency of service providers, availability of the required technology, infrastructure, and facilities.

Clinical Competence

The competence of service providers refers to their knowledge, skills, attitude, and actual practices. The clinical competence of medical professionals includes their ability to take the clients into confidence, diagnose their ailments correctly, and treat them appropriately. They should follow clinical protocols and advise only necessary diagnostic tests, medicines, and surgical interventions. The treatment should be completed in the shortest possible time. The outcome of the treatment should be consistent and in accordance with national or international standards.

Besides doctors, the nurses, paramedics, and support staff should also be competent in their work. For instance, a nurse should be skilled at establishing intravenous lines in patients with collapsed veins. She/he should be able to identify any adverse reaction to medicine or blood and manage it promptly. Similarly, the pharmacist should be able to explain how the prescribed medicines are to be consumed, their possible side effects, and warning signs, if any. The nurse aide should be able to assist an incapacitated patient with a bedpan and remove it, while ensuring minimum discomfort.

Technology, Infrastructure, and Facilities

To provide appropriate clinical care, service providers need the necessary technology, infrastructure, buildings, equipment, furniture, medicines, and other materials. The World Health Organization recommends the use of scientifically sound technologies with proven therapeutic value. Technology generally refers to the type of therapy, technical know-how, and required facilities. For example, it is a known fact that 10–15% of women end up with complications during pregnancy or child birth, most of which can be addressed by the prompt delivery of the baby through a caesarean section. So, a hospital that provides obstetric care should have round-the-clock surgical facilities. Surgical facilities imply the presence of a functional operating room with the required equipment, surgeon, anesthetist, nurses and operating room assistants, and sterile supplies.

Similarly, a hospital that caters to dengue fever cases should have the facility to diagnose dengue fever and rule out similar ailments. With dengue fever, there is the possibility that a patient's blood volume or platelet count will be reduced, which may result in bleeding through the nose, intestines, or elsewhere. Accordingly, there should be facilities for meticulously monitoring a patient's vital signs and blood volume and accurately maintaining the blood volume by administering appropriate amounts of fluids. In case platelets drop, there should be a facility for platelet transfusion.

Safety

Avedis Donabedian, a physician and quality expert, defined quality as the application of medical technology in a way that maximizes its benefits to health without correspondingly increasing its risks. Thus, Donabedian emphasized the safety of patients. Incidents of a drug or blood reactions, hospital-acquired infections, accidents, or complications from treatment should be minimal. The possibility of any such undesired effect should be explained to patients and their family members, and prior written consent should be obtained before surgery or an invasive procedure.

The safety of patients during their stay in a hospital is particularly important. A crash cart, life-saving medicines and supplies, a defibrillator, oxygen, a suction machine, and so on, should be available at all clinical service delivery points to manage medical emergencies. Advanced centers have a code blue protocol to call an emergency response team when required. Hospitals have to fight an ongoing battle to prevent hospital-acquired infections. A uninterrupted supply of electricity, water, oxygen, and vacuum is crucial for patients on ventilators or other mechanical devices. Disoriented or unconscious patients are to be protected from falling off beds by using bed railings. Patients can slip accidently in bathrooms, on stairs, or elsewhere. Similarly, mentally unstable patients can jump from windows or rooftops. Such issues are taken into consideration while designing the facility. Similarly, arrangements should be made to ensure that clients do not become trapped in elevators. There should be a well-defined and practical plan for evacuating bedridden patients in the event of a disaster like a fire or an earthquake.

Incident Management

Incident management is an important component of clinical care quality. Every untoward incident related to clinical care is to be reported and investigated by an expert, and the lessons from the investigation are to be disseminated to stakeholders with the aim of preventing similar incidents in the future. The entire process is to be documented.

Example: Guidelines for Incident Management in a Hospital

Any incidents causing harm to a patient or having the potential to cause harm that are attributed to hospitalization or clinical care are to be reported to a defined official of the organization. Examples of such incidents are

- An adverse reaction to a medicine or blood transfusion
- Hospital-acquired infection
- Complications, such as bed sores
- Accidents, for example, the fall of a patient from a bed or the fall of a patient in a washroom
- Any unnatural death

The nurse in charge of the ward or facility is required to report the incident in the prescribed format to a designated supervisor, say a deputy nursing superintendent, within an hour of the incident's occurrence (Figure 6.1).

The notification may be submitted online or through hard copy, depending on the level of automation in the hospital. If the nurse in charge is busy attending to other emergencies, she may inform the deputy nursing superintendent by telephone and may submit the form later when possible.

Upon receipt of the incident notification form, the deputy nursing superintendent will allocate a number to the incident. Then she will assign a senior nurse, who was not involved in the treatment of the client, to conduct a rapid investigation and submit a report, in the prescribed format, indicating the root cause of the incident and what actions need to be taken to prevent similar incidents in the future (Figure 6.2).

The deputy nursing superintendent will discuss the incident with the nursing superintendent. If the incident requires the medical director's attention, it will be brought to his notice. The nursing superintendent will present the incident, the findings, and the action plan in a monthly meeting with the senior management team of the hospital. The action plan will be finalized,

---

Incident notification form
Hospital A

- Name of the client: Mrs. X
- Age: 76 years
- Sex: Female
- Registration No. 2017/4/217
- Ward: (*There can be a drop-down menu*)
- Date of the incident: 17/04/2017
- Time of the incident: 1400 hrs
- **Type of the incident/Diagnosis:** (*Drop-down menu*)
  - ○ Adverse reaction to medicine
  - ■ **Adverse reaction to blood transfusion**
  - ○ Hospital-acquired infection
  - ○ Complication
  - ○ Accident
  - ○ Unnatural death
  - ○ Others
- **If others, specify**
- **Brief summary of how the incident occurred**
  The patient, a 76 years old female was operated for fracture of the left femur and the bone was fixed with a plate. The surgery was uneventful. She was shifted to post-operative recovery room, where blood transfusion was started. After sometime when she was stable, she was shifted to ICU. On the way, she started shivering. The patient was suspected to have developed reaction to the blood. Accordingly, treatment was provided and the patient became alright. The patient was shifted to ICU and her vitals were monitored closely and she remained alright
- **Category of the incident:** Drop down menu
  - ○ Death
  - ■ **Serious**
  - ○ Moderate
  - ○ Mild

- Name of the service provider and designation: Y, Nurse
- Incident notified by: Y, Nurse in ICU
- Date of notification: 17/04/ 2017
- Time of notification: 1540 hrs
- Incident No.   (to be assigned by the Deputy Nursing Superintendent):

Serious   : *Any incident that can cause threat to patient's life, limb, or organ.*
Moderate : *Any incident that does not pose any threat to patient's life, limb, or organ but requires specialized care.*
Mild   : *Any incident that did not pose any threat to patient's life, limb, or organ and did not require specialized care. It could be managed by the service provider on the site.*

Figure 6.1   Incident notification form.

and responsibilities will be assigned to prevent similar incidents in the future. The information about the incident and the required actions will be disseminated to all staff concerned through a formal mechanism, such as through email or by organizing a meeting with them or training them (Figure 6.3).

Incident Investigation Report
Hospital A

Incident No. 2017/ April/ 1
Date of investigation: 18/04/ 2017
Name of the investigating officer: Ms. M   **Designation:** Deputy nursing superintendent

Summary of the incident
A post-operative patient was put on blood transfusion in the post-operative recovery room and then while being shifted to ICU, on the way she developed reaction to the blood. The accompanying nurse could not identify the reaction immediately but a visitor of the patient identified that something is wrong with the patient and informed the nurse. The nurse rushed to the ICU and immediately got emergency medicines tray and administered injection adrenaline, injection chlorpheniramine maleate, and injection dexamethasone to the patient. The patient became alright within a few minutes. The patient was shifted to ICU and her vitals were monitored closely and she remained stable.

Things done well
1. Nurse accompanied the patient when she was shifted from post-op recovery to ICU
2. The nurse got the emergency medicines within 1-2 minutes of identifying the reaction and she could administer the required medicines immediately.

Reason for the incident
1. After starting blood transfusion in the recovery room, the patient was immediately shifted to ICU.
2. The patient, while being shifted developed reaction to the blood.
3. The accompanying nurse could not identify the blood transfusion reaction.

Root Cause (Drop down menu)
- **System's anomaly**
- **Provider's competence**
   ○ Provider's negligence
   ○ Others, specify

Recommended actions
1. To develop protocol: Patient should be shifted to another unit only after blood transfusion is over.
2. Refresher training of all nurses on identification and management of reaction to blood

Officer responsible for action: Ms. M, Deputy Nursing Superintendent
Date by which action should be complete: 30 April 2017
Officer responsible for closing the case: Ms. D, Nursing Superintendent

Signature of the officer closing the case   **Date:**

Figure 6.2   Incident investigation report.

The designated deputy nursing superintendent will follow up on decided actions and close the case when the required actions are completed.

Under the "no blame policy," the staff member that was responsible for the incident is not blamed. The name of the staff member concerned is not disclosed during the discussions. This is necessary to encourage the reporting of incidents and not their concealment. However, if a particular staff member is found to be responsible for many incidents of a similar

---

Memorandum

Date: 26 April 2017
From: M, Deputy Nursing Superintendent
To: All Assistant Nursing Superintendents

Subject: Training of nursing personnel on blood transfusion reaction

A discussion on 'Blood Transfusion Reaction' will be held with all assistant nursing superintendents on Saturday, 29 April 2017 from 4 to 5 PM in the conference room. We will discuss the following issues:

1. Common causes for blood transfusion reaction
2. Precautions to be taken before starting the transfusion
3. Identifying transfusion reaction
4. Managing transfusion reaction
5. Reporting, documentation

All are advised to come prepared for the discussion. Dr H from the department of anaesthesia will be the observer and resource person for this session.

Following the discussion, each assistant nursing superintendent will conduct a formal refresher training of all nurses in their wards on this topic. This would be done in batches to avoid disruption of work and to ensure that the nurses on off-duty also get the opportunity to participate.

After conducting the training, each assistant nursing superintendent will submit a report of the training to the undersigned by 28 April, 2017. The training report will include the date and timing of the training, list of participants, and topics of discussion. Any important issue or experience that came up during the discussions may be mentioned.

Signature
M
Deputy Nursing Superintendent

Figure 6.3   Action on learning from the incident.

nature, it is time to review his competency and performance. The entire process should be documented. An effective system for incident management is a requirement for securing the accreditation of the hospital.

It should be ensured that the process of incident management does not become a ritual. Each incident should lead to increased awareness by staff to prevent similar situations and improve systems.

Patient Satisfaction

The client should leave the facility with a positive experience after availing of services. Some clinical procedures or interventions can be painful or uncomfortable for the patient. Sometimes, medical professionals have to make a decision to amputate a body part or to go for a risky surgery. These decisions are made after weighing all possible pros and cons. Medical professionals are required to take a patient and his family members into confidence while making difficult decisions.

Interpersonal Communication

Interpersonal communication between a service provider and a client is an important determinant of the quality of patient care and plays an important role in determining client satisfaction. Service providers, by expressing their concern for the pain and suffering of the patients and showing an empathetic attitude, can earn their trust and confidence. Clients need to know about their problem, plan of treatment, prognosis, and expected expenses. In fact, it is their right. Medical professionals have a responsibility to provide them with this information from time to time. Service providers can further strengthen interpersonal relations with clients by listening to their problems and needs, and responding to them, if genuine. As discussed earlier, conflicts in healthcare settings are mostly due to interpersonal reasons, and most of them can be prevented if service providers are careful to communicate appropriately.

Ancillary Services

Despite good clinical care, in some hospitals, clients become dissatisfied due to the poor quality of ancillary services. For example, some patients are made to wait at the time of admission; they are made to wait to make various payments. Similarly, if the catering staff wants to retire early in the evening, they serve dinner early to admitted patients. Vigilant managers keep an eye on such issues and manage them appropriately.

Dignity, Privacy, and Confidentiality

Honoring the dignity of clients during the entire process of treatment is an important requirement of quality care. Maintaining privacy while interacting with clients or while examining them, and ensuring confidentiality of their personal information and records, are client rights and are important parameters for quality of care. Patient satisfaction is explained in detail in Chapter 7, this volume.

Measuring Quality

To improve quality, the first step is to decide what level of quality we desire. The second step is to measure the existing level of quality and identify gaps between the existing and desired situation. Efforts are made to fill the identified gaps. Step by step, the gaps are filled and improvements are measured. After achieving a level, the bar is raised and thus quality improvement is an infinite and ongoing process.

Quality can also be defined as conformance of services provided by a hospital or facility with predefined standards. We can measure the quality of patient care services in a hospital by determining the extent to which the services conform to a set of predefined standards. An organization can frame its own set of standards. It can also utilize the standards framed by an accreditation agency. Accreditation agencies develop a comprehensive list of standards for each department and service in a hospital. They can determine the extent to which the hospital adheres to those standards. If the agency is satisfied that the organization fulfills all quality standards, they provide accreditation.

Donabedian's Quality Framework

Avedis Donabedian, a medical practitioner and quality pioneer, in 1966, developed a systems framework that is still very relevant. This is also known as a quality framework. In this framework, the three major components of an organization are delineated as

- Structure
- Process
- Output

To achieve certain results or outputs in a hospital, we need to carry out specific activities or processes. To carry out those processes, we need some facilities or structure. In other words, structure leads to processes, and processes lead to output, as shown subsequently:

Structure
↓
Processes
↓
Output

Although we are primarily interested in output, the importance of processes and structure cannot be underestimated, as any flaw in them would eventually impact the output. Each component is further explained subsequently:

Structure

The structure of a hospital comprises

- *Infrastructure*: Adequacy and quality of buildings, lights, ventilation, uninterrupted electricity and water supply, drainage system, air conditioning
- *Manpower*: Adequacy of staff of each category, their competence and motivation

- *Materials*: Adequacy and quality of equipment, furniture, medicines, disposables, sterile supplies and other materials, systems for maintenance of equipment, systems for replenishment of consumables
- *Finance*: Adequacy of funds for the smooth functioning of the organization
- Policies, rules, regulations, standard operating procedures (SOPs), and clinical protocols

Processes

The processes in a hospital include

- *Clinical processes*: Outpatient consultations, inpatient care, intensive care, surgeries, diagnostic tests, emergency care, and clinical rounds in wards
- *Interpersonal processes*: Communication, behavior, and conduct of the staff
- *Managerial processes*: Client flow, flow of activities, supply chain management, human resource management, financial management, and marketing management

Output

The output of a hospital includes

- Number of patients treated, stabilized, or cured
- Patient satisfaction
- Profit earned by the hospital
- Number of deaths, complications, and hospital-acquired infections (these are undesired outcomes)

Output, in the long term, leads to "outcome." The outcome, in a still longer term, leads to "impact," as shown subsequently:

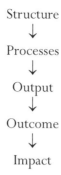

Structure
↓
Processes
↓
Output
↓
Outcome
↓
Impact

For example, the number of diabetic patients treated in a hospital is an "output" of the hospital services. Improvement in their quality of life of the treated patients is the "outcome." Improvement in the socioeconomic status of the entire community, as a result of the diabetic care services, indicates is its impact.

Operationalizing Quality Improvement

Commitment and Involvement of Leadership

Any quality improvement initiative needs the commitment of the organization's top management since it may require policy decisions, allocation of additional resources or staff time, which may not be possible without top management's support. However, eventually, the cost of care will reduce with quality improvement.

Kick-Starting the Program

Although involving every staff member of the organization is important in quality improvement initiatives, to kick-start the program, a small quality committee can be constituted. It may be led by a senior staff member who takes a special interest in quality improvement. One staff member from every major department can be a member of the committee. The leader provides direction to the team, coordinates their actions, and reviews progress. He also facilitates them receiving required support from top management.

Quality Standards

Quality standards are required to compare or measure the quality of services in the organization. Quality standards indicate the level of quality the organization intends to achieve. The committee decides the quality standards they would like to follow. A set of quality standards can be obtained from an accreditation agency. Two examples of quality standards in a hospital setting pertaining to outpatient clinics and inpatient services follow (Table 6.1):

For example, if a standard demands access of information to clients in the outpatient clinic, the quality committee members will define what information should be available to clients in the outpatient clinic area. They will prepare a document that provides all information that should be made available to clients. The document should be available in the front office. The quality team will also decide what information should be displayed prominently in strategic locations in the outpatient clinic. They will also develop guidelines for orientation and provide periodic updates to all concerned hospital staff on this information. Such documents and guidelines are important requirements of the accreditation process.

In the case of inpatient wards, if a standard demands emergency preparedness (Table 6.2), the quality committee defines what exactly will be available. For example, they may decide that there will be a crash cart in all nurse stations. They will list the nurse stations where crash cart should be made available. They list the medicines, equipment, and other supplies that should be available in each crash cart. They define the system for replenishment of supplies when they are used. They will also develop norms for training the nursing and

Table 6.1 Quality Standards in Outpatient Clinic

Standard	*Description*
Input	
Clients have easy access to outpatient clinics	The outpatient clinics should be located in a prominent location in the hospital and have easy accessibility from the road and from the main gate of the hospital. Wheel chairs and trolleys and hospital aides are available at the gate of the outpatient clinics to move the patient inside the clinic from ambulance or their personal vehicle
Clients have access to required information in the outpatient clinics	The front office staff in the outpatient clinic should be able to provide the following information to clients: • Availability of different services • Name of consultants based on specialty, their qualifications, clinic hours, consultation fee • Diagnostic tests available and their charges • Procedures available and their charges • Insurance information, third party administrator (TPA), package of services Information that is commonly sought by clients should be displayed prominently in the outpatient clinic area. There should be system to periodically update front office staff.
There is a defined system to manage client records	There is a defined system to provide outpatient records to clients, maintain a copy in hospital records department, and retrieve this when required. Routine client records should be preserved for a period of 3 years and medico-legal records for 5 years.

(Continued)

Table 6.1 (Continued)   Quality Standards in Outpatient Clinic

Standard	Description
Process	
Staff behave in a friendly manner with the clients	Staff should receive clients immediately upon their arrival. They should behave in a friendly manner and guide them through the next steps. They should inform them how much time it may take to receive a required service. There should be a system for periodic orientation of staff on soft skills. There should be a system to monitor staff behavior.
Consultants devote 10 minutes to each patient while providing consultation	Consultants should spend an average of 10 minutes with every new patient to record patient history, for examination, and to provide consultation
Consultants provide required information to every client about the illness/problem	Consultants should explain to every client the possible diagnosis, plan for investigation and treatment, possible outcomes or prognosis, and a rough estimate of expenses.
Output	
Client satisfaction is high	At least 95% of clients should be highly satisfied with the services in the outpatient clinic.

medical staff in emergency preparedness and emergency procedures. They may identify appropriate training materials, clinical guidelines, and protocols for staff training. They may define the system for monitoring and supervision of inpatient emergency preparedness.

Developing Common Understanding of Standards

The committee members need to develop a common understanding of the standards: What exactly each standard means and how it can be measured and achieved. The services of a consultant may be obtained to provide orientation for the

Table 6.2   Quality Standards in Inpatient Services

Standard	*Description*
Input	
There is a well-defined protocol for admission of patients	Clients should not be made to wait for bed allocation. If a bed is unavailable, the client should be referred to another hospital. When the client reaches the ward for admission, the bed should be ready. It should be provided immediately.
A nurse–patient ratio of 1:5 is maintained indoors	There should be one nurse for of every five clients in general wards
There are arrangements for dealing with emergencies in the wards	A crash cart should be available at each nurse station to deal with emergencies, if any. Staffs should be trained to manage emergencies.
Process	
Within an hour of admission, treatment of the patient should have started	Within 10 minutes of admission, a nurse should attend to the client and within half an hour a resident doctor should attend to the client. Required medicines should be available within an hour of admission and treatment started.
The condition of the admitted patient is monitored meticulously	The nurse should monitor the vital signs of the client and his response to the treatment every three hours and document the same in the client records. The consultant should visit admitted patients at least twice a day.
Medicines are administered to the admitted patient as per a prescribed schedule	The nurse should administer the prescribed medicines as per a prescribed schedule.

(Continued)

Table 6.2 (Continued)   Quality Standards in Indoor

Standard	Description
The personal hygiene of the admitted patient is maintained	The nurse, with the help of nurse aides, should take care of the personal hygiene of each patient. There should not be any delay in providing and disposing of bedpans. There should not be any delay in changing the linen of patient beds when required
An appropriate diet is provided to admitted patients	A dietician visits each admitted patient on the day of admission and whenever required and advises a diet keeping in view the patient's condition, the consultant's advice, and patient's likings.
There is a protocol for moving the admitted patient for investigations	For investigations that require moving the patient, a prior appointment is made, and the patient is moved accordingly along with his case records. Depending on the condition of the patient, a trained provider accompanies the patient.
Patients who are to undergo surgery are prepared for it	The nurse obtains the consent for the surgery. The nurse arranges for the pre-anesthesia check-up of the patient. The nurse prepares the patient for surgery as per the consultant's advice. The nurse arranges to shift the patient to the operating room as scheduled
Output	
Client satisfaction is high	At least 95% clients are fully satisfied with the indoor services.

committee members on these standards and to develop a common understanding.

Identifying Gaps in the Existing Services

Each team member can work in his department to identify gaps, if any, against the defined standards. The gaps are identified in reference to the structure, processes, and output.

Prioritization

If there are a large number of gaps, prioritization is an option. The gaps that are likely to endanger the safety of clients, affect clinical outcomes, or cause dissatisfaction among patients can be adopted as a priority in taking corrective actions.

Taking Corrective Actions

The thrust of corrective actions should be on improving systems and processes to ensure long-term sustainability. Complex issues may require a root-cause analysis to determine appropriate solutions. An action plan is developed to take corrective actions, and then it is implemented. Committee members should meet periodically to review progress in each department.

To sustain the program, the involvement of all staff members is necessary. Therefore, efforts should be made to engage them at various stages: While identifying gaps, while analyzing the root causes of the gaps, while determining solutions, and while taking corrective actions and reviewing progress.

Accreditation

An accreditation is a certificate stating that a healthcare facility has the required technical expertise and facilities to provide safe and effective services for specified types of health problems. Accreditation is usually a voluntary process, and there is no legal obligation for hospitals to obtain this. At the international level, the JCI provides accreditation. Many countries have their own accreditation boards. In the United Kingdom, the agency concerned is Care Quality Commission. In India, the National Accreditation Board for Hospitals and Healthcare Providers (NABH) is the nodal agency providing accreditation to hospitals.

Process of Accreditation

Hospitals wishing to receive accreditation can purchase a copy of the standards from the accreditation agency. They can conduct a self-assessment against those standards and identify gaps, if any, and take corrective actions. When they are confident of their compliance with the standards, they can submit an application to the accreditation agency requesting accreditation. Upon receiving the application, the agency assigns a pre-assessment team led by a principal assessor to visit the hospital and assess the degree to which the hospital conforms to the standards. If the team finds gaps, it recommends suitable corrective actions. When the hospital confirms, having taken the corrective actions, the agency again organizes an assessment. If the visiting team is satisfied with the compliance, they make a recommendation and the agency provides the certification. The accreditation certificate is valid for a specific period, say 3 years. For renewal, the hospital is required to submit a new application to the agency, which organizes another assessment. The agency reserves the rights to withdraw or suspend the certification upon finding any irregularity in adhering to quality standards.

Quality Standards in Public Health

We provide a few examples of quality standards in community-based health programs. Diarrhea and acute respiratory infections are the two most common causes of death in children in economically poor regions. Simple technologies are available to identify and treat these diseases in primary healthcare settings. Tables 6.3 and 6.4 illustrate how the quality of services can be improved in primary healthcare settings.

Table 6.3 Standards for Management of Diarrhea in Children in a Primary Healthcare Facility

Standard	Description
Input	
All service providers are trained in diagnoses and treatment of diarrhea in children	All service providers should have undergone formal training in diarrhea management in children
Service providers have the required means and facilities to diagnose and treat diarrhea in children	Service providers should have the required equipment to examine a child: a watch (with second's hand), thermometer, pediatric stethoscope, and blood pressure gauge. They should have adequate supplies of oral rehydration salt packets and the means to demonstrate preparation of oral rehydration solution (ORS).
All service providers have access to a referral center	All service providers should be aware of a referral hospital, and they should have the contact information of their counterpart in the referral center. They should have access to transportation to move the child to a referral center.
Process	
All service providers are competent in treatment of diarrhea in children	All service providers should provide ORS to the mothers of children with a history of diarrhea. They should demonstrate the process of preparing ORS solution. They should guide the mothers in administering ORS to the child. They should advise continuation of breastfeeding or normal feeds to the child. They should educate the mothers on signs of dehydration/warning signs in children.

(Continued)

Table 6.3 (Continued)   Standards for Management of Diarrhea in Children in a Primary Healthcare Facility

Standard	Description
All service providers are competent in diagnosing dehydration in children and promptly refer the patient to the referral hospital	All service providers should be able to diagnose dehydration by checking the patient's history and examining the child. They should be able to promptly refer a child with signs of dehydration for intravenous therapy.
Output	
Reduction in child mortality due to diarrhea	Deaths of children due to diarrhea should stop occurring in the region.
Client satisfaction is high	At least 95% of clients should be highly satisfied with the services provided to them by the health workers.

Table 6.4   Standards for Management of Acute Respiratory Infections in Children in a Primary Healthcare Facility

Standard	Description
Input	
All service providers are trained in diagnoses and treatment of acute respiratory infections (ARI) in children	All service providers should have undergone formal training in ARI management in children.
Service providers have the required means to diagnose and treat ARI in children	Service providers should have the necessary equipment to examine a child: a stop watch (with second's hand), thermometer, pediatric stethoscope, and blood pressure apparatus. They have amoxicillin suspension, amoxicillin dispersible tablets, syrup paracetamol, and so on, for treatment of ARI in children.
All service providers should have access to a referral center	Service providers should be aware of the referral hospital, and they should have the contact information of the concerned staff in the referral center. They should have access to transportation to move the patient to the referral center when needed.
Process	
All service providers are competent in diagnosing ARI in children and prescribing appropriate treatment	All service providers should be able to diagnose ARI through history taking from the mother/caregiver and examining the child, particularly measuring the respiratory rate. They should be able to prescribe the right dose of amoxicillin preparation or other antibiotics as needed. They should be able to guide the mother in administering medicine to the child properly.

(Continued)

Table 6.4 (Continued) Standards for Management of Acute Respiratory Infections in Children in a Primary Healthcare Facility

Standard	Description
All service providers are competent in identifying danger signs of pneumonia and promptly refer the patient to the referral hospital	Service providers should be able to identify warning signs of pneumonia, that is, rapid or difficulty in breathing, dehydration, high-grade fever, inability to accept food, and so on. Service providers promptly refer the patient to the appropriate referral center.
Output	
Child mortality due to ARI is reduced	Deaths of children due to ARI and its complications should reduce significantly.
Client satisfaction is high	At least 95% of clients should be highly satisfied with the services they received.
Mothers' awareness of ARI management in children is improved	Mothers should become aware of the risks of ARI in children and the danger signs.

Bibliography

World Health Organization (WHO), *Quality of Care: A Process of Making Strategic Choices in Health Systems*, WHO, Geneva, 2006.

National Accreditation Board for Hospitals and Healthcare Providers (NABH), *Standards for Hospitals*, 3rd edn., Quality Council of India, New Dehli, 2011

Chapter 7

Patient Satisfaction

Patient satisfaction is an important indicator of the quality of care in a hospital. A hospital manager's foremost concern is to see that the clients are fully satisfied when they leave the hospital. Many patients who face inconveniences in the hospital avoid lodging a complaint. As a result, many shortcomings in the hospital services go unnoticed by the management. Therefore, it is important for managers to proactively identify gaps in service delivery and take corrective measures. In this chapter, we will discuss common issues that cause dissatisfaction among patients, and explore ways of addressing them.

In this chapter, we have used the generic terms "patient" and "patient satisfaction" for all sorts of clients.

Patient Expectations

What do patients expect when they visit a hospital? It is interesting to note that several studies conducted in different types of hospitals, in different countries, came out with similar findings. They all concluded that patients expect

1. Prompt attention
2. Concerned service providers
3. Correct diagnosis and treatment
4. Amenities, such as a decent waiting area, cleanliness, toilets, water, and food
5. Affordability of services

How to Enhance Patient Satisfaction

Patient satisfaction can be enhanced by fulfilling their expectations. Some of the issues that need to be addressed are

Delays

Undue delay in receiving services is the most common cause of dissatisfaction among patients in hospitals. From the point of entry to exit; a patient has to wait at many points, such as the registration desk, doctor's office, laboratory, and pharmacy. In a busy hospital, everyone understands that they cannot receive immediate service if there are already people waiting. But, even if after waiting patiently for quite some time they see people jumping the queue, they become disappointed and develop a negative impression of the hospital. To prevent patient dissatisfaction on this account a system of "first come first served" needs to be implemented strictly.

The front office staff can play an important role in reducing patients' anxiety by providing information, such as how many patients are already waiting prior to them, and when they can expect their turn. The staff can guide them to the waiting area. If the waiting time is too long, they may suggest they visit the cafeteria and come back before the expected time of appointment. The digital display of a patient's "call information" is very useful. It may also be made available in the cafeteria. In some hospitals, physician assistants inform each patient individually when their turn comes.

It is not uncommon to see front office staff talking on the telephone while patients are waiting. It is quite natural for a person to respond to a telephone call, dropping everything else. While multitasking is good, patients who are present in front of the staff should be their first priority. Separate staff should be appointed to answer incoming calls at the back of the front office. Sometimes front office staff lack complete information about the hospital services or they are not proficient in retrieving the information from a computer, this slows down the process at the front office. Since staff turnover is high in many hospitals, there should be a system for updating and training staff on a regular basis.

The following information is commonly sought by patients at the front office:

- About consultants—their outpatient days, schedules, availability for appointment, consultation fees, and ward round schedules
- Availability of different services, diagnostic tests, surgeries, and other procedures
- About insurance claims
- Availability of beds or rooms for admission, their categories, facilities in each category, and tariffs
- Procedure for admission, amount to be paid in advance at the time of admission
- Cost of different services, estimates, and packages of major procedures
- Location of different departments and services
- Whereabouts of an admitted patient
- Information about hospital staff members

The front office staff should also be updated on dynamic information, such as the unavailability of a staff member due to his involvement in an emergency case, or due to his availing of leave. For any additional information, staff should have access to a senior or experienced colleague. Information

commonly sought by patients should be displayed in a prominent manner in the waiting area or lobby to reduce patients'
dependence on the front office. Similarly, adequate signage
and direction boards can save time for everyone.

In private hospitals, most of the patients have prior appointments, yet sometimes they are made to wait. This is often
because of consultants running late. In such a case, front
office staff should have the authority to contact consultants
and learn about their whereabouts and when they will be
available. Accordingly, the patient should be informed of the
delay and given a new time slot.

In the case of an admitted patient, his family members tend
to get worried when the patient does not receive the prescribed medicines or when an intravenous fluid bottle is not
replaced promptly. For them, prompt administration of medicines is critical to the patient's recovery; whereas, a short delay
does not make much of a difference to service providers.

Example 1: A patient was admitted for surgery. On the
morning of the surgery the anesthesiologist recommended an
echocardiogram to assess the patient's fitness for anesthesia.
This required moving the patient to the echocardiography
room, but the ward aides were busy elsewhere; so, the nurse
could not arrange to move the patient. Meanwhile, the family members of the patient were worried that if the test was
not carried out promptly, the surgery would be postponed. As
a result, they kept reminding the nurse. The nurse, who was
busy with an emergency, became irritated and responded in
an inappropriate manner causing client dissatisfaction.

Solution: In such a situation, the nurse should have provided the reason for the delay and the time when she would
be able to move the patient. She could have also assured them
that the surgery would not be postponed, if the test results
were normal.

When a treating consultant advises discharge to an admitted patient, the patient and his family members become
impatient to return home at the earliest possible time. They

are required to clear their bills and collect a discharge summary before leaving. The discharge summary is prepared by a resident doctor who generally does so after finishing his other assignments. The patient's family members keep reminding the nurse to secure the discharge summary, but she feels helpless in fulfilling their need. Either there should be an arrangement to prepare the discharge summary whenever needed or the treating consultant should give a time of discharge that takes into account the time required to prepare the discharge summary. Wherever possible, standards should be formulated for important activities. An example of a standard may be that within 60 minutes of a consultant's advice for discharge, the patient will be provided with the final bill and discharge summary. Compliance with standards can be improved by displaying them at relevant places in the hospital.

Staff Behavior

Inappropriate behavior by hospital staff is the second most common reason for patient dissatisfaction. Many service providers, working in hospitals for a long period, become insensitive to the pain and suffering of patients. In our medical and nursing schools, not much emphasis is placed on behavioral aspects. Traditionally, senior doctors do not show much concern for patients, and this is emulated by the other staff. Medical professionals, particularly doctors and nurses, must express their concern for the patient. Doctors are often in a position to assure patients that they will receive the best possible treatment. This inspires a feeling of trust and confidence in patients and their family members. And this should be done without giving any false assurance or hope. The behavior of every staff member matters, be it the security guard at the parking lot, the elevator operator, the admission desk officer, the housekeeping person, the pantry boy, the nurse, the doctor, or the billing clerk. Any staff member who comes in contact with clients should be sensitized to behavioral aspects.

This can be done by organizing role-play exercises in a class-room setting, followed by on the job support. Conflicts in hospitals occur when some of the staff members behave inappropriately with patients. Dissatisfied patients are more likely to question their bills. It is worth emphasizing here, that if the hospital staff is courteous and caring, patients may be willing to ignore many shortcomings in the delivery of services. This is, however, not to suggest that there should be any deficiencies in the service.

It is important for hospitals to recover the cost of services, but that should not be done by unfair means. For example, there have been instances when the management of a hospital instructed its nurses not to remove discharged patients' cannula until their bills were cleared.

Clinical Care

Sometimes when an expensive investigation or a procedure is suggested to a patient, they doubt whether it is really necessary or if the doctor has a vested interest in it. It is not always possible for patients to judge the appropriateness of an investigation or treatment suggested to them. Certain procedures, though expensive and uncomfortable, could be essential to a patient's recovery. Patients generally become worried when their condition does not improve or it further deteriorates. An explanation by the doctor on why particular tests are needed or why a patient's condition is not improving can be helpful in alleviating the patient's anxiety. Increasing communication with patients is the key to increasing patient satisfaction.

Amenities

Diet

It is a common belief in India that when a person is sick, he should not eat normal meals; a patient should eat something light. But that is not always right. Many admitted patients are fit to have a normal meal. In fact, a bedridden patient may have nothing pleasant to look forward to except a delicious meal. A dietician should meet each patient individually to understand their dietary requirements and preferences. Providing appropriate and delicious food and beverages to patients in a hospital can contribute a great deal to enhancing their satisfaction. It is a low hanging fruit for hospital managers.

Before major surgeries or procedures, patients are required to fast overnight. Sometimes when a surgery is postponed, the patient is not informed and he continues fasting unnecessarily. It is only when the patient's hunger becomes unbearable and family members approach a nurse or doctor, that they learn that they are allowed to eat. Such negligence on the part of hospital staff keeps going unnoticed. They need to be conscious of such issues.

Toilets

Unclean toilets are a common complaint in hospitals that must be taken care of. Close monitoring is necessary to ensure that the admitted patients do not face any problems in getting bedpans or disposing of them promptly.

Disturbance to Patients in Rooms

Service providers keep moving in and out of patients' rooms for various reasons, such as recording vital signs, administering medicines, serving food, clearing dishes, cleaning rooms, clearing dustbins, and changing linen. Sometimes this can cause too much of a disturbance to patients, particularly if they are in severe pain or agony. Therefore, staff members should be conscious to work gently and cause the least disturbance to patients. Wherever possible, they may carry out some of these activities jointly.

Cost

Many medical professionals are of the opinion that people are not willing to pay for their treatment even though they spend lavishly on their comforts and luxuries. They may not be aware that it is not uncommon for people to sell their property for the treatment of their family member. In rural India, medical expenses are the most common cause of financial burden and indebtedness for people. Patients who are treated expeditiously and with care tend to be less concerned about the cost of their treatment; the cost becomes important, primarily, when people find gaps in the quality of the care they receive. As mentioned earlier, if the staff members are courteous and caring, patients are often willing to ignore many shortcomings in the services.

Exceeding Patient Expectations

Management can make clear to staff members that merely meeting the expectations of patients is not enough; they should try to exceed client expectations and earn their trust. A mid-level manager may meet each admitted patient at least once during their stay in the hospital, determine their satisfaction, and ask if anything else could be done for them. Patients are likely to appreciate such a gesture. Patients often lose or spoil their case file or discharge summary. Some of them have loads of papers in their file. It may be a good practice to hand over all documents to them labeled and tagged systematically with a decent file cover at the time of their discharge. If possible, a comprehensive summary should be provided so that the patient does not have to carry so many documents for review. Making a telephone call to patients a few days after their discharge to inquire about their health and how they are doing, and making a call to remind them of any follow-up are good practices. Managers need to devise innovative ways to please patients.

Satisfying Internal Clients

The staff of an organization constitute its internal clients. Dissatisfied internal clients are unlikely to make any effort to satisfy the external clients. If the work environment in an organization is polluted by factionalism, favoritism, inappropriate competition, and disharmony and if the staff members do not have an exciting career path to look forward to, they are likely to remain demoralized. Securing staff members' commitment is not easy; effective organizational development interventions are required to get staff members' commitment.

While it is important to ensure that hospital staff members treat the patients well, it is equally important to protect staff members' dignity. Staff members should not be allowed to feel helpless at any stage.

Assessing Patient Satisfaction

Patient satisfaction can be assessed through the following methods:

- Complaint tracking
- Exit interviews
- Telephone surveys
- Input from staff members

Each method has its merits and demerits. Adopting more than one method can be advantageous.

Complaint Tracking

Common complaints made by patients are

- Delay in getting a service
- Rude behavior by staff

- Information not provided about a patient's condition, plan of his treatment, projected expenses, and prognosis
- Incorrect diagnosis
- The consultant did not attend to an admitted patient when required or requested
- Negligence by doctors or nurses; side effects or drug reactions not identified
- Medicine not administered as per schedule
- Unnecessary tests or procedures carried out
- Referral not made on time
- Poor amenities, such as unclean toilets, bed sheets not changed when soiled, bedpan not provided or removed promptly, no place for family members to sit while waiting
- Excessive or unreasonable cost of services
- Billed for services that were not actually provided
- Not allowed to meet an admitted patient

Even when dissatisfied, many people avoid making a formal complaint. Some people do not want to express a negative opinion while they are on the hospital premises or under treatment. Verbal complaints made by a patient to some of the hospital staff often go unrecorded and unreported to the management. In many organizations, patients do not have easy access to senior managers.

Suggestion boxes can be installed in the waiting areas of a hospital to provide an opportunity for clients to give suggestions or make complaints. They should have the option to not disclose their identity. There should be a system to open the boxes regularly, collate the collected information, and inform the officials concerned. Complaint tracking or suggestion boxes cannot measure patient satisfaction; however, they can be an additional source of information.

Exit Interviews

Patients are requested to fill a questionnaire at the time of their discharge. This is a common method used in many hospitals for assessing patient satisfaction and getting their suggestions. To reach a definite conclusion, it is important to have a statistically adequate sample. It should also be noted that staff might avoid asking dissatisfied clients to fill the questionnaire. Nevertheless, the findings of exit interviews can reveal trends of patient satisfaction for specific services.

Telephone Surveys

Telephone surveys are a reliable source of information if the interviewers are skilled. People are generally more open to expressing their feelings over the phone, especially if the time of the call has been fixed according to their convenience. They can explain how they felt about various services and can provide valuable suggestions for improvements.

Input from Staff Members

Staff members who deal with patients day and night, often have an in-depth understanding of the problems patients face, their satisfaction level, and what can be done to improve services. This is a valuable source of information, which is often not utilized by many organizations.

Focus Group Discussions

Focus group discussion (FGD) is a special method of data collection used in qualitative research. It can be used in a hospital setting to understand staff members' perceptions about patient satisfaction. The success of an FGD depends on identification of the right issues and appropriate framing of questions. And, more importantly, on the skills of the facilitator in encouraging participants to give their frank opinion and respond to a contrary opinion given by another participant. A group of about 6–8 staff members can participate in an FGD and they can be from different cadres. The discussion should be conducted in a common area, say a meeting room, and the FGD may last for about an hour. The responses of the participants are carefully recorded by another person.

To begin the discussion, the facilitator asks the participants for their opinion on a particular service; in their opinion, how satisfied are the patients? Participants who feel that patients are satisfied with that service give their opinion and share their experiences. Similarly, participants who have a different opinion share their experiences. The facilitator ensures that the FGD is not limited to questions and answers. He encourages the participants to discuss among themselves to make their point, argue, and counterargue with a person who has a different opinion, and eventually reach a consensus. The facilitator plays a crucial role in keeping the discussion focused. Several issues can be introduced one after another. If conducted skillfully, an FGD can provide valuable information about which the authorities may be ignorant.

Special Considerations in Designing Patient Satisfaction Studies

Patient satisfaction depends not only on the quality of services provided to patients in a hospital but also on many extraneous factors as explained subsequently:

Patients with serious or malignant diseases or irreversible conditions are less likely to be satisfied with the hospital care. This is quite understandable since many patients are not able to come to terms with their condition, or they may believe that there is a definite cure for their problem, which is not being provided to them. Accordingly, in a tertiary care hospital, patient satisfaction can be low as a large proportion of their patients have advanced problems and complications. Therefore, while selecting a sample for assessing patient satisfaction, a mix of cases with different levels of severity should be included.

A patient's perception can change over time. On the day of the surgery, a patient may feel low because of excruciating pain. He may be uncertain about the outcome of the surgery. He may even feel lonely in the intensive care unit where he is not able to meet his family members. He may be worried about the hospital expenses. But, after a few weeks or months, after recovering fully, he may forget the pain and suffering of the procedure. He may appreciate the expertise of medical professionals and the care provided to him. Therefore, the researcher should take these factors into account when interpreting the results.

In a study, it was found that patients who selected a hospital themselves were more satisfied with its services in comparison to those who visited the hospital on someone's recommendation. Another study found that patients were more satisfied in government hospitals than in private hospitals. On further exploration, it was found that this difference was not because of a higher quality of services in government hospitals but because of the lower expectations of their patients. Patients are generally more dissatisfied with the behavior of nurses than doctors. This is because nurses are in contact with patients for a longer time. Besides, patients have higher expectations of them.

Patient satisfaction surveys only include respondents who avail of services from the hospital. Some patients leave the hospital against medical advice without completing their treatment. They are likely to be highly dissatisfied but they will not be included in the study because of the challenge involved in tracking them down. In addition, there may be people who reside near the hospital but avail of services elsewhere. They or their family members might have had a bad experience with the hospital. These are some of the limitations of patient satisfaction studies.

How to Manage Patient Dissatisfaction

Any complaint from a patient demands careful analysis to understand its root cause and to take corrective actions. We tend to believe that problems in organizations are mostly due to the incompetence or poor attitude of staff members. But, this may not always be correct. Most cases of patient dissatisfaction are the result of weaknesses in hospital systems and not because of the staff. Therefore, it is important to carefully identify gaps in the hospital systems and fix them. If dissatisfaction persists, it may then be appropriate to identify the individual with deficient skills or personality issues. It is often possible to change a staff member's behavior through one-on-one discussions. Complaints from patients or results of patient satisfaction surveys that provide evidence of a staff member's lower performance can be shared with them. An individual is likely to feel disturbed upon learning that his performance is below that of his colleagues based on well-defined criteria. Such individuals are likely to work to improve their standing to put it on a par with their colleagues'.

Bibliography

Mayor Salluzzo and Kidd Strauss, *Emergency Department Management: Principles and Applications*, Mosby, 1st edn., 1997.

Chapter 8

Mission, Vision, and Values

Mission, vision, and values provide direction to an organization. They may also play a role in attracting potential clients.

Mission

The mission of an organization indicates the very purpose of its existence; what it is trying to achieve and how. A hospital's mission statement generally indicates what type of services it provides, for example, single-specialty or multispecialty, and to whom. Some hospitals highlight the expertise of their professionals or the quality of care that they provide, while others stress the affordability of their services. Some hospitals underscore their intention to promote the wellness of people, extending to home care. The mission of Johns Hopkins Hospital is to improve the health of its community and the world by setting the standard of excellence in patient care. Specifically, it aims to be the world's preeminent healthcare institution and provide the highest quality care and service for all people in the prevention, diagnosis, and treatment of human illness. It also aims to attract and support physicians and other health care professionals of the highest character and greatest skill and to be the leading health care institution in the application of discovery.

The work of Marie Stopes International, a healthcare organization, is based on the mission: children by choice, not chance. It provides family planning and reproductive health services to prevent unwanted births in underserved communities in several countries. The mission of EngenderHealth, an international nongovernmental organization (NGO) is to improve the health and well-being of people in the poorest communities of the world by strengthening the capacity of healthcare service providers.

Vision

The vision of an organization indicates its ambition: how it intends to grow in the long term, say in 5 or 10 years. For example, a hospital has the vision to become the largest and most sought-after nephrology center in the city in the next 5 years. A 100-bed hospital desires to establish a chain of 10 satellite hospitals with a total capacity of 500 beds within a span of 10 years.

The vision of Marie Stopes International is a world in which every birth is wanted.

Values

Some healthcare organizations claim to value "client interest" as the foremost consideration in all their dealings and business. An example of this is a hospital with these stated values: "We are open to all people who need our care and our time." The values adopted by an organization enrich its culture and influence the way its staff deals with clients.

Strategic Management

Organizations achieve their mission and vision through strategic management. If there are several options available to an organization to achieve its objectives, the option it adopts is known as its "strategy." Strategic management is also known as strategic planning. It is the long-term planning of an organization. It charts the direction for an organization. It defines an organization's desired future state and the means of achieving it. It includes making crucial decisions on the allocation of resources.

For example, the mission of a hospital is to provide eye care to all those who need it, regardless of their capacity to pay; and its vision is to be the most respected high-tech ophthalmology institution in the state. The management of the hospital would try to achieve its mission and vision through the process of strategic management. The hospital may consider adopting the strategy to cross-subsidize poor patients by the rich. It may not opt to raise donations or establish ties with corporate entities based on corporate social responsibility. The hospital may decide to utilize surplus money to hire higher-level ophthalmology experts and acquire the latest equipment. It may contemplate starting a postgraduate course in ophthalmology to raise the level of expertise in the institution. To become the most reputed eye hospital, management may decide to put in extra resources and effort into quality improvement.

Chapter 9

Planning

Planning is the process of deciding what we want to achieve and how we intend to achieve it. It may involve making assumptions and answering questions before they arise.

Business Plan

Before making an investment, a business plan is prepared to determine the feasibility of a proposed project and the expected returns. Based on the findings, one can make the decision to invest or not. A business plan explores the factors that are known to determine the success of a project. A typical business plan includes the following sections:

1. Market analysis
2. Scope of the proposed services
3. Organizational capacity
4. Projected financials
5. Statutory requirements

Market Analysis

What is the market that we intend to tap? In other words, market analysis involves identifying the people who may require our services? What is the catchment area and the size of the target population? What are their needs? "Need" is the starting point of any business. People are likely to accept and use those services that can fulfill their needs and expectations. And that is critical for the success of any business, and its sustainability. For example, economically poor communities may need healthcare services for safe deliveries, immunization, and the management of diarrhea or pneumonia in children. Economically better off communities may require facilities for the management of diabetes and facilities for angiography and angioplasty. The youth may need services for vision correction, prevention of unwanted pregnancies, or protection from HIV/AIDS. Wealthy women may use cosmetic surgeries. A geriatric population may require facilities for cataract surgery, cancer, or long-term care. The needs and expectations of a community can be determined through special studies known as "need assessments" or "situational analyses." A typical need assessment study collects the following information:

- Size of the target population
- Breakdown of the target population: male, female; children, adults, elderly
- Literacy levels
- Means of livelihood and economic status
- Lifestyles
- Health awareness
- Prevalent health problems
- Health-seeking behavior
- Expectations from healthcare organizations
- Paying capacity
- Other health care providers or competitors in the area, their services, and coverage

Scope of Proposed Services

Taking into account the needs and expectations of the people in a community and their willingness to pay, we can consider offering certain services. For example, in some countries, in higher economic strata, there is a huge demand for knee replacement services. Knee replacement surgeries are available in the orthopedic departments of large multispecialty hospitals. To be competitive, we may consider establishing a stand-alone, high-tech joint replacement center. We may offer a competitive package and a special package for two joint replacements together. Further value can be added by providing services of specially trained physiotherapists to visit a patient's home until they can walk independently. This service may be part of the package. Better amenities may be provided in the hospital and a relationship may be maintained with the clients on a long-term basis.

Organizational Capacity

After having conceptualized the services that we intend to offer, we need to assess the capacity of our organization to provide those services. SWOT (strengths, weaknesses, opportunities, threats) analysis is a management technique to assess the strengths and weaknesses of an organization.

SWOT Analysis of a Hospital

A hospital may have certain strengths in terms of highly competent orthopedic surgeons, state-of-the-art operating rooms, credibility in the community, and a large client base. Its weaknesses might be limited space for further expansion, high turnover of nurses, or unrest among staff. Further, the SWOT analysis explores the opportunities and threats in the environment that may influence the organization. Opportunities might be better health-seeking behavior or the increasing paying capacity of people. The increasing prevalence of osteoarthritis in the region might be an opportunity for a hospital to set up a joint replacement center. Similarly, the increasing prevalence of diabetes in a community is an opportunity to provide diabetic care services. Threats might include competition from another hospital in the area. It might be useful to map existing or upcoming hospitals in the region that might be competitors. We can also obtain information on their strengths and weaknesses. It would be of particular interest to know what gaps in their services cause client dissatisfaction. Accordingly, we can take special care to address them in our services. We need to be alert to changes in government policy that may adversely affect the hospital's profitability. Increasing public distrust in medical professionals can also be a threat.

SWOT Analysis of a Community-Based Healthcare Organization

The strengths of a community-based healthcare organization may be its competent service providers, trainers, or outreach workers. Its outreach may have spread to remote and hard-to-reach areas. It may have a strong link with grassroots-level nongovernmental organizations (NGOs) or civil society. An NGO may be weak due to a lack of sustained funding.

Projected Financials

"Return on investment" is an important consideration for an investor. While planning a new project, we work out the total investment required and make projections on the expected returns. Investment in a project includes capital costs and recurring expenses.

Capital costs are one-time expenses incurred for purchasing land, building infrastructure, equipment, and other assets.

Recurring expenses are on staff salaries, electricity, maintenance, marketing, and consumables. Secondly, projections are made for the expected returns or revenues or income from the services. These are based on the proposed unit cost of each service and the number of clients expected to utilize each type of service. Assumptions can be made in this regard. Over time, we expect an increase in the utilization of services, and this aspect can also be factored into calculations. The break-even point is the point at which the total cost of the project and total revenues become equal and there is no net loss or gain. The profits begin to accrue from that point. Investment decisions are made on such financial projections.

On commissioning of services, the recurring expenses start while the financial returns may not be certain. For example, the employed staff must be paid salaries whether services are utilized or not. Similarly, electricity, housekeeping, and many other expenses will keep occurring. Therefore, the organization needs funds to meet the "running expenses" or "fixed cost" to manage the show until the time expected revenue returns start accruing.

In big projects, when the investments are huge, organization may consider leveraging funds from external sources through loans or equity. In that case, the interest on the loan amount is added to the recurring expenses.

Some community-based healthcare organizations receive funds from donors like USAID, the Bill and Melinda Gates Foundation (BMGF), DFID, or the Packard Foundation. These donors are interested in improving the health status of a community and in the sustainability of program activities. Financial returns are of no consideration to them. Some corporations set up their own foundations to carry out philanthropic work. Some healthcare organizations partner with corporations under their corporate social responsibility (CSR) schemes to implement health programs.

Statutory Requirements

It is important to know the relevant government regulations and to obtain the necessary approvals before starting a venture to avoid legal hassles and to save the project from getting stuck midway. For example, to establish a new hospital in India, registration under the state's Clinical Establishment Act is required. A license is required from the Atomic Energy Regulatory Board to install and operate radiation emitting X-ray and CT scan machines. The Chief Controller of Explosives of the government of India provides a license for the installation of an oxygen tank and to use compressed or liquefied medical gases on hospital premises. The central or state Drugs Standard Control Organization provides drug licenses for retail dispensing of medicines through a hospital pharmacy. In addition, there are statutory requirements for fire safety, pollution control, biomedical waste disposal, sewage and drainage systems, and installation of elevators, which should be complied with. Medico-legal procedures should be followed diligently, and their records should be prepared carefully and stored safely. In case a patient dies during the course of treatment in hospital, the hospital manager should be well-versed in the legal procedures.

Healthcare organizations that receive funding from outside the country have to follow certain regulations, for example, in India, they are required to register under the Foreign Contribution Regulation Act (FCRA) and submit quarterly reports of their remittances and expenses to the government and upload this information to their website. International healthcare organizations intending to work in India are required to register as an Indian entity. Another option for them is to obtain permission from the Reserve Bank of India to work as a liaison office. A liaison office is not allowed to earn any income within the country. It is required to meet its expenses through remittances from its head office.

An Example of a Business Plan

An entrepreneur, interested in investing in a hospital or health-care project, learned about inadequate dialysis facilities in the region. He got a needs assessment study done, which revealed that the geriatric population in the region has been increasing for the last three decades resulting in a higher need for dialysis services. Many super-specialty hospitals were built in the region in recent years, but with limited dialysis facilities. As a result, there were long waiting lists for dialysis in the existing hospitals. The entrepreneur thought of utilizing the business opportunity.

He came up with the idea of establishing a stand-alone dialysis center on a plot of land of 2400 square feet. The center would have 10 beds and 10 dialysis machines. It was decided that the facility would operate in two shifts of 8 hours each. There would be two medical officers, two nurses, and two nurse assistants on each shift. It was planned that the facility would function on Sundays and holidays also. Accordingly, positions for two leave reserve nurses and two assistants were included in the plan. A decision was made for the medical officers to be the managers during their shifts and one of the nurses on duty to receive the clients and settle their bills. Other support services like housekeeping, security, and maintenance were to be provided on contract.

It was learned that the complete process of dialysis for a patient takes about 4 hours, which means one machine can provide dialysis services to a maximum of two clients in one shift and to four clients in a day. Therefore, working at full capacity, 10 machines would be able to serve 40 clients a day, 1,200 clients a month, or 14,400 clients a year.

On the modest side, it was projected that in year 1, the use of services would be at 50%, which would increase to 70% in year 2, and 90% in year 3.

During the dialysis process, certain consumables are used. The expenses of these consumables vary with the number of dialysis services provided. These are known as variable costs. The cost of electricity also varies with the usage of machines but may be ignored being minor in nature. Other recurring expenses like staff salaries, housekeeping, and security will remain the same irrespective of the number of the clients served. These are known as fixed cost.

Projected financials are explained in subsequent sections.

Expenses

Capital Cost

The projected capital costs on purchase of land, construction of buildings, interiors, equipment, and furnishing are given in Table 9.1.

Table 9.1   Capital Cost of Setting up a Dialysis Unit

S. N.	Item	Units	Unit Cost ($)	Amount ($)
1	Land cost	2,400 sq. feet	Lump sum	500,000
2	Construction cost	1,200	35	42,000
3	Interiors	1,200	18	21,600
4	Dialysis machines	10	12,000	120,000
5	Reverse osmosis unit	1	10,000	10,000
6	Patient beds	10	160	1,600
7	Bedside lockers	10	80	800
8	Office furniture	1 set	Lump sum	2,000
9	Mattress, pillow, blanket, bed sheets, other	10 sets	200	2,000
10	**Total capital cost**			**700,000**

Budget Notes

1. A plot of land having an area of 2400 square feet will be purchased at a cost of $500,000.
2. The cost of construction of a building with a covered area of 1200 square feet is estimated at $35 per square foot amounting to $42,000.
3. The cost of interiors and decoration is estimated at $18 per square foot amounting to $21,600.
4. Ten dialysis machines, each costing $12,000, will be purchased for $120,000.
5. One reverse osmosis unit is estimated to cost $10,000.
6. Ten patient beds cost $1600.
7. Ten bedside lockers cost $800.
8. Other office furniture, including one table and fourteen chairs are estimated at a lump sum cost $2000.
9. Ten mattresses, 10 pillows, 10 blankets, 50 bed sheets, and 50 pillow covers (5 sets of bed sheets and pillows) are estimated to cost $2000.
10. Thus, the total capital costs for the project are estimated to be $700,000.

Recurring Expenses in Year 1

In the first year, it is projected that the utilization of services will be 50% of its capacity serving 600 clients. Projected recurring expenses for the first year are given Table 9.2.

Budget Notes

1. Two medical officers, each at a monthly salary of $2,000 will cost $48,000 per year.
2. Six nurses, each at a monthly salary of $800 will cost $57,600 per year.
3. Six nurse assistants, each at a monthly salary of $400 will cost $28,800 per year.

Table 9.2 Year 1: Recurring Cost

S. N.	Item	Units	Unit Cost ($)	Monthly Expenditure ($)	Annual Expenditure ($)
1	Salary for medical officer	2	2,000	4,000	48,000
2	Salary for nurses	6	800	4,800	57,600
3	Salary for nurse assistants	6	400	2,400	28,800
4	Consumables (with 50% uptake)	600	25	15,000	180,000
5	Electricity expenses			1,500	18,000
6	Water expenses			20	240
7	Housekeeping services			1,200	14,400
8	Security services			600	7,200
9	Maintenance services			500	6,000
10	**Total**			**30,020**	**360,240**
11	Miscellaneous @ 5%			1,501	18,012
12	**Recurring expenses**			**31,521**	**378,252**
13	Depreciation				33,800
14	**Total recurring expenses**				**412,052**

4. It is estimated that each dialysis will need consumables worth $25. In the first year, for 600 dialysis the cost of consumables will be $15,000 a month or $180,000 a year.
5. Electricity is estimated to cost $1,500 per month and $18,000 per year.
6. The cost of water is estimated at $240 per year.
7. Housekeeping services will cost $1,200 per month and $14,400 per year.
8. Security services will cost $600 per month and $72,000 per year.
9. Maintenance services including an annual maintenance contract (AMC) for equipment and infrastructure maintenance will cost $500 per month or $6000 per year.
10. Total recurring costs for the above items are estimated to be $30,020 per month or $360,240 per annum.
11. An amount of $18,012 at 5% of recurring expenses per year is earmarked for miscellaneous or unforeseen expenses.
12. By adding miscellaneous, the recurring cost comes to $378,252 per year.

Depreciation

On the assumption that the life of dialysis machines and reverse osmosis plants is 5 years, depreciation is estimated at 20% of the cost of equipment per year. Infrastructure and furniture depreciate at 10%. It is expected that the mattresses, blankets, bed sheets, and pillow covers will last for 2 years, accordingly; they depreciate at 50% of their purchase value. Total depreciation amounts to $33,800 per year as shown in Table 9.3. This will be valid for 2 years. Since the cost of mattresses and so on will be fully charged off in 2 years, from the third year onwards, the depreciation will reduce to $32,800.

There is no depreciation in the value of land.

Thus, the total recurring expenses in the first year (including depreciation) is projected to be $412,052.

Table 9.3 Depreciation of Capital Goods

S. N.	Item	Amount ($)	Rate of Depreciation (%)	Amount of Depreciation ($)
1	Land cost	500,000	Nil	0
2	Construction cost	42,000	10	4,200
3	Interiors	21,600	10	2,160
4	Dialysis machines	120,000	20	24,000
5	Reverse osmosis unit	10,000	20	2,000
6	Patient beds	1,600	10	160
7	Bedside lockers	800	10	80
8	Office furniture	2,000	10	200
9	Mattresses, pillows, blankets, bed sheets, etc.	2,000	50	1,000
10	**Total**	**517,700**		**33,800**

Recurring Expenses in Year 2

In year 2, operating at a capacity of 70%, 840 clients are expected to receive services per month. By accounting for 10% annual increment in staff salaries and 10% increase in costs of electricity, housekeeping, maintenance, and consumables. (depreciation remaining the same), the recurring expenses in the second year are projected to be $527,745 (Table 9.4).

Recurring Expenses in Year 3

With a further 10% rise in salaries and the costs of other services, the recurring expenses in year 3 are projected to be $670,035 as shown in Table 9.5.

Table 9.4   Year 2: Recurring Cost

S. N.	Item	Units	Unit Cost ($)	Monthly Expenditure ($)	Annual Expenditure ($)
1	Salary for medical officer	2	2,200	4,400	52,800
2	Salary for nurses	6	880	5,280	63,360
3	Salary for nurse assistants	6	440	2,640	31,680
4	Consumables	840	27	22,680	272,160
5	Electricity expenses			1,650	19,800
6	Water expenses			22	264
7	Housekeeping services			1,320	15,840
8	Security services			660	7,920
9	Maintenance services			550	6,600
10	**Total**			**39,202**	**470,424**
11	Miscellaneous @ 5%			1,960	23,521
12	**Recurring expenses**			**41,162**	**493,945**
13	Depreciation				33,800
14	**Total recurring expenses**				**527,745**

Table 9.5   Year 3: Recurring Cost

S. N.	Item	Units	Unit Cost ($)	Monthly Expenditure ($)	Annual Expenditure ($)
1	Salary of medical officer	2	2,420	4,840	58,080
2	Salary of nurses	6	968	5,808	69,696
3	Salary of nurse assistants	6	484	2,904	34,848
4	Consumables	1,080	30	32,400	388,800
5	Electricity expenses			1,815	21,780
6	Water expenses			24	290
7	Housekeeping services			1,452	17,424
8	Security services			726	8,712
9	Maintenance services			605	7,260
10	**Total**			**50,574**	**606,890**
11	Miscellaneous @ 5%			2,529	30,345
12	**Recurring expenses**			**53,103**	**637,235**
13	Depreciation				32,800
14	**Total recurring expenses**				**670,035**

Income

Keeping in view the prevailing market price of $50–$60, the promoters of this plan thought of keeping the price of one dialysis service at $50 in year 1 and increasing it to $55 in year 2, and $60 in year 3.

Table 9.6 shows projected income of $360,000 in year 1, $554,400 in the year 2 and $777,600 in the year 3.

Income–Expenditure

Based on this income, a deficit of $52,052 is projected in year 1. However, in year 2, a surplus of $26,655 is projected, which is expected to increase to $107,565 in year 3 (Table 9.6).

Breaking Even

As previously noted, the project is expected to yield a surplus in the second year. However, if we take into account the deficit of the first year, the surplus is pushed to the third year (Table 9.7).

To determine the exact break-even point, we need to calculate the minimum number of dialysis services that would meet the recurring expenses. With an increase in the number of services, profit will begin to accrue.

We can manipulate the unit price of services or the uptake of services to check at what level breaking even can be achieved.

From Table 9.8, we can see that by increasing the unit price to $57.30, we can breakeven in the first year if the utilization of services remains the same. Alternatively, we can try increasing utilization to 57.3%, that is 8251 dialysis services, and can thereby breakeven in year 1.

Profitability

To set up this business, the promoter has to bring in a minimum of $1,112,052, which includes the capital cost ($700,000) and, the recurring expenses of the first year ($412,052). In the third year, when the project starts functioning at an optimal capacity of 90%, it is expected to yield a return of $82,168 per annum. So, the return on investment will be about 7.4%. It may not be a very attractive business proposition for some of the investors.

Table 9.6 Summary of Income–Expenditure in Years 1–3

Years	Projected Uptake of Services (%)	Projected Service Units/Year	Recurring Expenses ($)	Unit Price of a Service ($)	Annual Income ($)	Profit/Loss ($)
Year 1	50	7,200	412,052	50	360,000	−52,052
Year 2	70	10,080	527,745	55	554,400	26,655
Year 3	90	12,960	670,035	60	777,600	107,565

Table 9.7   Commencement of Profit

Years	Recurring Expenses ($A)	Deficit from Previous Year ($B)	A + B	Income ($)	Net Deficit/ Surplus ($)
Year 1	412,052	0	412,052	360,000	−52,052
Year 2	527,745	−52,052	579,797	554,400	−25,397
Year 3	670,035	25,397	695,432	777,600	82,168

Table 9.8   Effect of Manipulation of Unit Price or Uptake of Services on Profit/Loss

Projections	Projected Uptake of Services (%)	Projected Number of Services	Unit Price ($)	Income ($)	Profit/ Loss ($)
Year 1: Initial projection	50	7,200	50	360,000	−52,052
Option 1: Increasing the cost of unit service	50	7,200	57.3	412,560	508
Option 2: Increasing use	57.2	8,251	50	412,560	508

Secondly, if the promoter borrows money for the investment, he will have to pay the interest which will further
reduce profits and prolong the break-even stage.

Thus, with the help of such financial projections, an investor can make wiser investment decisions.

Goal and Objectives

Once a decision to set up a business is made, the proposed
project's goals and objectives are defined. In management

parlance, this approach is known as "management by objectives." A goal indicates a broad intention. It can be broken down into several small objectives. For instance, the goal of a project is to set up a stand-alone joint replacement center. Its objectives may include, engaging four renowned joint replacement surgeons, establishing two state-of-the-art operating rooms, and a ten-bed intensive care unit. The goal and objectives of a project provide clarity on what exactly will be achieved.

Example: In some communities, girls get married at an early age and produce children, resulting in poor health outcomes and sometimes even deaths. In this context, the goal of a healthcare project was to increase girls' age at marriage in a specific community. Project objectives included increasing awareness of the community on the minimum legal age of marriage; tracking and re-enrolling girls who drop out of school; organizing vocational training for out-of-school adolescent girls; organizing pre-marriage counseling; and promoting registration of marriages.

Developing an Action Plan

After a decision is made to go ahead with a project, an action plan is prepared, which is also known as the program implementation plan (PIP). The action plan lists the activities required to accomplish the goals and the objectives of the project. It also specifies the individuals who will be responsible for each activity and sets a timeline. To establish a new hospital, an action plan may include the following activities:

- Land acquisition
- Architectural drawings
- Civil work, sanitary and plumbing work, electrical and air conditioning work
- Procurement and installation of equipment

- Hiring of human resources
- Commissioning of services

The Gantt chart is a simple yet very useful management control device to depict an action plan. It is a simple horizontal bar chart that shows the beginning and end of each activity. At a glance, it shows the chronological relationship of the activities and where they overlap. It also specifies the individual responsible for each activity (Table 9.9).

Developing Microplans

Each major activity in the action plan is further detailed out in microplans. To hire personnel, for example, the following sub activities would be required:

- *Determining human resources requirements*: Listing various categories of personnel required in the proposed hospital, such as doctors, nurses, technicians, ward assistants, housekeeping staff, security personnel, front office staff, electricians, and managers. The doctors can be senior consultants, junior consultants, resident doctors, and general duty medical officers. Similarly, different levels of nurses and other staff are determined. The human resource requirements of different service areas, such as outpatient clinics, inpatient rooms, operating rooms, and the intensive care unit are determined. Heads of departments and some other key positions can be engaged at an early stage to utilize their services in planning and recruiting other staff. After finalizing the human resources requirements, the job responsibilities of each cadre are defined, followed by the following activities:
- Posting an advertisement in newspapers or websites, or contracting a placement agency

Table 9.9   Gantt Chart: Planning a Joint Replacement Center

Activity	Responsible Officer	Q1	Q2	Q3	Q4	Q5	Q6	Q7	Q8
Land acquisition	Owner/ investor	▓							
Architectural drawings	Architect	▓							
Engineering work	Chief engineer		▓	▓					
Sanitary and plumbing work	Chief engineer			▓	▓				
Electrical, water, air conditioning work	Chief engineer			▓	▓				
Procurement and installation of equipment	Manager-materials					▓	▓	▓	
Procurement of drugs and other supplies	Manager-materials							▓	
Hiring of HODs/key positions	HR manager				▓				
Hiring of other human resources	HR manager						▓	▓	
Marketing of services	Marketing manager			▓	▓	▓	▓	▓	▓
Commissioning the services	CEO								▓

Note: Q1–8 are quarters (3-month-period).

- Receiving applications and short listing candidates
- Conducting telephone interviews
- Conducting personal interviews, skill tests, personality tests
- Selecting candidates and setting salaries
- Issuing offer letters and providing job descriptions
- Acceptance by candidates
- Induction training
- Placement
- Setting up a system for staff reviews

Some services, like housekeeping and security, can be contracted out.

Similarly, for the procurement of equipment, we need to work out the types of equipment needed in each department, the quantity, and specifications.

Furthermore, the microplans are executed to achieve the objectives and the goal of the project.

An Example of Planning a Healthcare Project

Maternal and child health indicators in the Bihar province are among the poorest in India. A philanthropic foundation decided to invest to improve the situation. The foundation selected an international NGO to execute the project. The NGO had expertise in women's and children's health. After preliminary discussions, the foundation asked the NGO to first pilot its strategies in a poor performing district of the province and scale up if the results were promising. The foundation asked the NGO to submit a proposal.

The international NGO conducted a rapid study and submitted the following proposal in September 2007:

Proposal

Improving Health Practices of Mothers in Marginalized Communities in Gaya District in Bihar, India

Background

India accounts for the largest number of maternal deaths in the world. There is marked variation among different provinces and districts. Bihar is one of the poorest performing states in India. While the maternal mortality ratio is 212 in India, it is 261 in Bihar (Sample Registration System, 2007). In Bihar, Gaya is one the poorest performing districts, having a maternal mortality ratio of over 300.

Similarly, the infant mortality rate is very high, at 61, in Bihar and mortality for under-fives is 84 (National Family Health Survey-3).

The poor health practices of women are important reasons for this situation. In addition, poor access to quality healthcare services adds to the problem. Some of the health practices of women that adversely affect maternal and child health indicators are

1. Women getting married before the age of 18
2. Women becoming pregnant or becoming mothers by 19 years of age
3. Married women (15–49 years) not using any modern method of contraception
4. Women not getting antenatal checkups in the first trimester of pregnancy
5. Women not consuming iron folic acid tablets during pregnancy
6. Women not having all four antenatal visits during pregnancy
7. Women not opting for institutional deliveries
8. Newborns not being breastfed within an hour of birth
9. Children not exclusively breastfed for 6 months

10. Children not fully immunized
11. Children not receiving measles vaccine
12. Children, on having an episode of diarrhea, not treated with ORS and zinc

Aim

The project aims to reduce maternal, infant, and child mortality and improve their health by improving the health practices of mothers in Gaya district.

Objectives

1. Improve awareness of mothers on health practices and encourage them to adopt the same.
2. Advocate with the state and district health systems to improve mothers' access to healthcare services.
3. Generate demand for healthcare services.

Strategy

The project will aim to improve women's awareness of health practices and encourage them to practice these. It will also generate demand for healthcare services.

This will be done through village-level volunteers, who will be specially trained for this purpose.

The achievements of the project will be measured through specially conducted surveys. Also, comparisons will be made with the findings of national family health surveys and annual health surveys.

Geographical Coverage

Gaya district is divided into 24 blocks. In each block, there are about 80–200 villages. Due to a limitation of resources, the project proposes to make interventions in selected villages from each block with the expectations that promising practices will spread to surrounding areas through word of mouth. From each block, the 20 most backward villages will be identified. In each village from the marginalized communities, a group comprising of about 10 women of reproductive age will be formed. The group will be mentored by a village-level trained volunteer.

Implementation Plan

From each intervention village, a young woman volunteer will be identified to form a group of women of reproductive age from marginalized communities. The volunteer, known as a "friend" will educate them on health-related practices. The criteria for selection of volunteers will be

1. Tenth-level standard qualified or ability to read and write
2. Good oral communication skills
3. Good reputation in the village
4. She should be willing to visit the women of reproductive age in her village
5. She should be confident forming a group of about 10 women who will assemble at a common place in the village to attend educational sessions
6. She should have good training skills
7. She should be able to document educational activities

Preference will be given to a women from marginalized communities, but this is not mandatory. The project will be implemented only in those villages where a suitable volunteer is available and willing to participate in the project.

The identified women volunteers will be provided with intensive training on healthy practices, communication skills, and training skills. After the training, they will be asked to form a group of women of reproductive age in their village and conduct participatory sessions with them on identified topics. Suitable training materials and job aides will be prepared in local languages and provided to them. The volunteers will get a nominal remuneration for each educational session they conduct.

Why will volunteers take the initiative to educate women in their village? Firstly, it will satisfy their needs for self-esteem or leadership, and secondly, they will get a nominal remuneration for each educational session they hold.

Monitoring and Evaluation

The village-level volunteers will be supervised and mentored by block coordinators. The block coordinators will be supervised by a district coordinator.

Six monthly surveys will be conducted to assess the awareness and practices of women on the defined indicators.

The survey findings will be corroborated with the national family health survey and annual health surveys conducted by the government of India.

Expected Results

It is expected that there will be significant improvement in the health-related practices of women in Gaya district and, accordingly, after 5 years of interventions, maternal, infant, and under-fives mortality will be reduced by at least 30% each.

Project Team

The organization will set up an exclusive team for executing this project. The team will be led by a project manager. The following four specialists will assist the project manager:

1. Capacity-building specialist
2. Demand-generation specialist
3. Monitoring and Evaluation (M&E) specialist
4. Finance/admin officer

For implementation of the project at the field level, there will be five program coordinators: one for every five blocks.

Each program coordinator will supervise about five block coordinators. Thus, there will be 24 block coordinators. Each block coordinator will supervise and provide support to 20 village volunteers.

An office will be set up at the district headquarters. The program coordinators and block coordinators will work from home.

For training of village volunteers, the capacity-building specialist will organize and prepare training modules for trainers and for participants on the following topics:

1. Antenatal care
2. Safe delivery practices
3. Immunization of children
4. Management of diarrhea and acute respiratory infection (ARI) in children
5. Hygiene and sanitation

These modules will be translated into the local language, that is, Hindi and pretested. Pedagogy will involve participatory discussions, roleplay, and demonstrations. The participants will be declared successful only if they are able to reproduce the contents accurately during the practice training sessions.

The village volunteers will be trained in batches of 20 participants at the district headquarters. Five hundred volunteers will be trained in 25 batches. After successful training, each volunteer will form a group of women in her village and organize educational sessions for the group. Thus, 500 women will be oriented. In the initial stages, the village volunteers will conduct supervised sessions and once a block coordinator certifies their effectiveness, will the volunteer be allowed to conduct further sessions. The volunteers will maintain a record of the sessions.

Table 9.10 Project Budget

S.N.	Item	No. of Units	Unit Rate ($)	Monthly Expenses ($)	Annual Expenses ($)
1	Project manager	1		3,125	37,500
2	Project specialists	4		2,000	96,000
3	Project coordinators	5		800	48,000
4	Block coordinators	24		500	144,000
5	Village volunteers	500		40	240,000
	Total of salaries				**565,500**
6	Office expenses			2,000	24,000
7	Laptops	10	400	4,000	4,000
	Total of office expenses				**28,000**
8	Development of training modules	5	2,000		10,000
9	Printing of modules	2,500	2		5,000
10	Training expenses	500	100		50,000
	Total of training expenses				**65,000**
11	Travel of district office staff	5	150	7,500	90,000
12	Travel of field staff	30	50	1,500	18,000
13	International travel	2	10,000		20,000
	Total of travel expenses				**128,000**

(Continued)

Table 9.10 (Continued) Project Budget

S.N.	Item	No. of Units	Unit Rate ($)	Monthly Expenses ($)	Annual Expenses ($)
14	Staff monthly meetings	12	1,000		12,000
	Total of meeting expenses				**12,000**
	Total				**798,500**
	Overhead s @ 25%				199,625
	Grand total				**998,125**

Budget

Refer to Table 9.10 for budget.

Budget Notes

Salaries of the Project Staff

1. The project manager at a monthly salary of $3,125 will cost the project $37,500 annually.
2. Four project specialists, each at a monthly salary of $2,000 will cost $96,000.
3. Five project coordinators, each having a monthly salary of $800 will cost a total of $48,000.
4. Twenty-four block coordinators, each at a monthly salary of $500 will cost $144,000.
5. About 500 village volunteers will be engaged in the project. Their payments will be based on the number of sessions conducted by them. For each session, they will be paid $10. They will be paid for a maximum of 4 sessions in a month. Thus, volunteers will cost a maximum of $240,000 per year.

The total expense for salaries of project staff will be $565,500.

Office Expenses

1. A lump sum of $24,000 on office rent, housekeeping, electricity, and so on, has been budgeted per year.
2. Ten laptops for the project manager, four specialists, and five program coordinators are estimated to cost $4000.

Thus, the total office expenses will be $28,000 per year.

Training Expenses

1. To develop training modules, the support of consultants will be used, which may cost about $2,000 per module and a total of $10,000.
2. The printing of 2500 copies of 5 modules will cost $5000.
3. Each of the 500 village volunteers will be trained at a cost of $100 each, costing $50,000.

Thus, the total cost of training is estimated to be $65,000 per year.

Travel Expenses

1. Travel for five head office staff to supervise and monitor is estimated at $150 per month each, costing a total $90,000.
2. Travel for program coordinators and block coordinators is estimated to cost $18,000.
3. A sum of $20,000 is budgeted for international travel by two staff.

Thus, total expenses for travel will be $128,000.

Meeting Expenses

1. It is expected that every month a staff meeting will be held that will incur expenses for the travel of participants, the venue, and working lunches, amounting to $12,000.

The total cost for these expenses comes to $798,500.

The cost of the overhead at 25% will be $199,625.

The grand total after adding the overhead will be $998,125.

Thus, the project will cost about 1 million dollars per year.

Approval

The philanthropic foundation asked the NGO to reduce the overheads to 15% and resubmit the budget. After the NGO submitted a revised budget, the foundation approved the proposal and the budget and gave a go ahead to execute the project.

Chapter 10

Organizing

When several people work collaboratively toward achieving a common goal, they constitute an organization. Hospitals and nongovernmental organizations (NGOs) are a type of organization. The process of "organizing" comprises bringing together various resources to set up functional units and establishing relationships between them. In other words, organizing involves two broad functions:

- Developing a structure
- Delineating relationships

Developing a Structure

The structure of an organization includes its land, buildings, human resources, furniture, equipment, medicines, and other assets. These resources are organized in relation to one another to set up functional units. Functional units are also known as systems.

When setting up a hospital, the owner needs to decide whether it will be a single-specialty or multispecialty hospital, and what size hospital it will be: how many beds, how many

133

operation theaters, and how many intensive care beds, and what level of expertise will be available. In the following sections, we will discuss the nuances of setting up a hospital as an organization.

The major functional units in a hospital setting are

- Clinical services
- Support services
- Human resources
- Finance and accounts
- Materials
- Marketing

Patients visit a hospital primarily for diagnosis and treatment. Clinical departments provide these services.

Clinical Services

Clinical services include broad specialties and super specialities. Broad specialties are: medicine, surgery, gynecology-obstetrics, pediatrics, orthopedics, eye, ear nose and throat (ENT), skin, and psychiatry. Super specialities include cardiology, neurology, and oncology.

In a hospital, services are delivered through the following outlets or facilities:

- Outpatient clinics
- Emergency department
- Inpatient department
- Intensive care units
- Operation theaters
- Radiotherapy department

Medical, nursing, and paramedical professionals provide clinical services.

Clinical departments are dependent on support and utility services to function.

Support Services

Clinical departments require the support of laboratories, X-rays, and CT scans for diagnosing problems in patients. Facilities, such as a pharmacy, blood bank, and medical gases provide support to clinical departments in treating patients. They all constitute support services.

Certain services, such as the front office, admission desk, medical stores department, housekeeping, and ambulance services are not directly involved in diagnosis or treatment, but they are necessary for the smooth functioning of a hospital. They constitute utility services.

Organizing Outpatient Services in a Hospital

As an example, we will now discuss how outpatient services can be organized in a hospital. Discipline of management advocates: Function determines structure and not vice versa, which means that the design of a facility should be based on the functions it intends to perform or the services it intends to provide. The outpatient department provides the following services:

■ Providing information and registering patients
■ Providing clinical consultations
■ Conducting diagnostic tests
■ Supplying medicines

To carry out these functions, the following facilities are set up:

■ *Reception/registration desk*: To provide information to clients and register outpatients

- *Waiting area*: For patients and accompanying visitors to sit while waiting for a consultant
- *Doctors' offices*: For doctors to examine the patients in privacy and provide consultations
- *Laboratory collection center*: To collect samples from patients for diagnostic tests
- *Radiology*: To take X-rays or other imaging investigations
- *Pharmacy*: To supply medicines
- *Amenities*: Drinking water, toilets, cafeteria, ATM, and so on

Each facility requires resources like a room or space in the building, staff, furniture, equipment, and other supplies. The requirements of human resources can be estimated based on the expected client load, and the quantum of work done by one person in one shift. The physical resources required by each staff member are determined; for example, a billing clerk would require a workstation, a computer with an accounts and billing module/software, access to online patient data, and a printer to provide receipts for payments, as well as a cash box to keep cash and return any balance amount to the clients.

Flow of Activities

Facilities are organized in relation to one another to create a seamless flow of patients and activities. For example, the help desk and registration desk are set up near the entrance. Further away, consultants' office are set up. A waiting area is organized outside the consultants' office. There can be a large central lobby and small waiting areas in front of each office. Earlier, when patients were advised that they needed laboratory tests, they were required to go to the laboratory, which used to be elsewhere. Nowadays, a sample collection room is set up within the outpatient clinic area, and that makes it very convenient for the patients. The radiology department is set up closely so that fracture and arthritis cases can get imaging tests conveniently. Similarly, the billing desk and pharmacy are also set up within the clinic area.

In addition to streamlining the patient flow, the flow of supplies and the flow of information are also to be organized. For example, how sterile supplies will be replenished in the gynecologist's chamber should be defined. Similarly, how cash collected by a billing clerk and deposited with the finance department when his shift is over should also be defined.

Now we will take up the example of a community-based healthcare organization and discuss how its organization can be set up. Depending on the objectives of the project undertaken by the organization and the available funds, an intervention area is defined: which province and how many districts. Staff requirement and level of expertise required at various levels is determined. Decisions are made: where each staff will be positioned at the district, block, or village level. Decisions are made on how many offices will be established and their locations. In some projects, some staff members are allowed to work from home. The logistics and other support required by each staff to perform his functions are determined. The mechanism for their supervision is determined. The requirements of support staff to manage finance, administration, and logistics are determined. Thus, a structure is designed and created, and this process is known as organizing.

Delineating Relationships

Once the structure of an organization is set up, the relationship between its people has to be delineated. Conflicts are often caused by ambiguity in the roles and responsibilities of staff members. Frequent conflicts are obviously detrimental to the smooth functioning of the organization. Policies, rules, regulations, protocols, and guidelines delineate relationships between staff members, and they define channels of communication. The following tools or processes are useful in this regard:

Organization chart: An organization chart or organogram displays the hierarchy and line of command of the organization—who is senior and who reports to whom. In some hospitals, the heads of clinical services, support services, human resources, finance, and marketing are all top-level managers and are of equal status. They all report to the CEO. In some hospitals, the materials manager is a top-level manager, while in others, he is a mid-level manager. An organization chart clarifies such issues.

The organogram of hospital-1in Figure 10.1 shows that the hospital is headed by a CEO. Four directors report to him: the director of medical services, director of finances, director of HR and director of administration. All of them are of the same level. The head of nursing services reports to the director of medical services.

In hospital-2 (Figure 10.2), the director of nursing services and the director of medical services are at the same level. In such a situation, the nursing services are expected to grow faster and develop higher expertise. However, in this case, the CEO has the additional responsibility of supervising the nursing director. Also, there can be resentment from medical professionals, who often want nurses to be their subordinates.

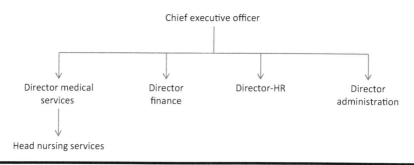

Figure 10.1 Organogram of hospital-1.

Figure 10.2   Organogram of hospital-2.

It is for the top management or governing board of an organization to decide how they would like a speciality or department to develop.

Delegation

A manager cannot do everything on his own; he has to delegate some of his responsibilities to his deputies. In fact, a
traditional definition of management is: It is the art of getting work done through others. Some people believe that
doing something on your own is easier than getting it done
through others. And that is the challenge faced by managers.
The head of clinical services is responsible for all the clinical
functions of the hospital. He delegates the responsibilities of
managing clinical departments to the heads of departments,
who further delegate the responsibility of the clinical care of
patients to consultants. In case of negligence in the treatment
of a patient, the treating consultant would be held responsible. Thus, responsibilities and accountability are handed over
down the line.

It should, however, be understood that delegation of a
responsibility does not absolve a manager of his accountability
for the same. If there are many cases of medical negligence in
a hospital, although the treating consultants would be responsible for the individual cases, the head of clinical services
will also have to answer for having failed to set up systems
to check such eventualities. Similarly, if there are many cases
of embezzlement of hospital funds, the cashier concerned
will not be the only one responsible, the head of the finance

would also be accountable for having failed to devise ways to prevent this.

During the process of delegation, responsibility and authority go hand in hand. Authority refers to the power of an officer to make a decision. Managers at different levels are provided with different authority. For example, the clinical head may have the financial power to purchase equipment up to a certain amount. If the cost of equipment exceeds his financial power, a higher authority, that is, the CEO's approval would be required. If the cost is even beyond the power of the CEO, the management board's approval will be required.

Delegation is one of the most neglected management functions. This is because of a general misconception that handing over one's responsibilities to others is not a big deal; anyone can do it. But that is not correct. It needs to be understood that delegation is a highly skilled function and one has to learn it on the job. It requires internalizing the fact that delegation does not limit a manager's control and power. At the same time effective delegation empowers subordinates, enhances their capacity to perform, and boosts their morale. Common reasons for under-delegation are

- Lack of experience in delegating
- Desire for excessive control or perfection
- Distrust in subordinates
- False assumption that delegation will be interpreted as a manager's inability to perform the task
- Fear that subordinates will resent having so much work delegated to them

On the other hand, some managers over delegate and burden their subordinates, who may resent this. Some managers delegate without providing the required information or resources; some delegate power to the wrong person. Both under- and over-delegation adversely affect an organization's performance and the staff's morale.

Division of Labor

The process of distributing work among the employees of an organization or a unit is known as "division of labor" in management parlance. For example, in the materials management department, one manager may be responsible for making the purchases, and the others may be responsible for managing stores. There may be several sub stores, such as the medical store, linen store, OT store, and general store. Each sub store may be headed by an in charge. Similarly, to ensure cleanliness in a large hospital, the entire floor area of the hospital can be divided into small units that can be supervised by one housekeeping supervisor. He will further divide his area for each housekeeping staff. Thus, for the cleanliness of each unit area of the hospital, a specific housekeeping staff as well as a specific supervisor would be accountable.

Job Responsibilities

The job responsibilities of each person in the organization should be defined, documented, and made known to all concerned. For example, there have been instances of pregnant women passing stool on the labor table resulting in conflict between housekeeping staff and hospital aides. The housekeeping staff believes that his job is to clean the floor of the room. He thought cleaning the equipment and labor table was the hospital aide's responsibility. On the other hand, the hospital aide thought that he is required to do the dusting of the equipment and not cleaning fecal matter. Clear job responsibilities are necessary to avoid such conflicts.

Guidelines

For each important task in the hospital, a point person should be responsible and accountable. For example, the condition of an admitted patient deteriorated and the consultant found that the patient did not get the medicines that he was prescribed. The ward nurse reported that she had placed the requisition with the hospital pharmacy but did not receive the medicines. The pharmacist reported that the medicines were not available in the hospital pharmacy. In this situation, who would be held responsible? The nurse is responsible for the treatment of the patient. She should know what actions she has to take when a patient under her care does not get the required treatment or care. She could have informed the consultant, who could have prescribed alternate medicines. On the other hand, the pharmacist could also have arranged to get the medicines by making an urgent local purchase. Well-defined guidelines can help prevent such situations.

When the structure of an organization is in place and relationships between different players are delineated, it is ready to start its operations.

Chapter 11

Monitoring and Supervision

Monitoring and supervision are an integral part of the process of implementation of a program. These days, the term "operations management" is commonly used, it is akin to monitoring and supervision. Monitoring and supervision aim to identify deviations, if any, from the established plan and to find quick, practical solutions to bring the activities back to the predefined track. Although "monitoring" and "supervision" are two distinct terms, they are often used together and carried out by the same supervisor or manager. However, for conceptual clarity, the subtle difference between the two should be understood. Monitoring focuses on activities, and supervision focuses on personnel. That means, a manager supervises the personnel and monitors the activities performed by them. In supervising, the manager needs to be present on the spot to observe the staff members performing their jobs, to interact with them, assess their knowledge, and seek their opinion. However, the manager can monitor their performance remotely by reviewing their service statistics and reports. In this chapter, the terms "manager" and "supervisor" are used interchangeably. In the health sector, expressions such as "supportive supervision" or "facilitative supervision" are commonly used with the intent of supporting the staff to perform better rather than finding their faults.

Job of a Supervisor

Before assessing the performance of a staff member, a supervisor or a manager should first ensures that the staff

1. Is competent to perform his job
2. Has the required materials and logistic support to carry out his job
3. Is motivated to achieve the desired results

These are the prerequisites for staff to perform.

Methods of Monitoring and Supervision

Managers employ the following methods for monitoring and supervision:

1. Observation
2. Communication with staff
3. Communication with clients
4. Review of records

Observation

Example 1: In an outpatient clinic of a hospital, a manager observed the help desk staff interacting with clients. He was trying to determine whether the staff members were able to provide the required information. However, he noticed that the staff members were not very courteous and friendly with the clients. After the clients were disposed of, he guided the staff on behavioral aspects and reiterated that the staff members are expected to behave in a friendly manner with all clients. He also considered organizing a short orientation program on soft skills for all front office staff.

Example 2: In a community-based healthcare program, a manager supervised as outreach workers conducted awareness-generation sessions in a village. After the talk and discussions, they also distributed oral rehydration salt to the mothers of children who had diarrhea. A manager observed the session and felt that the mothers did not get adequate information on preparing the solution properly. He felt that there should also be a demonstration on the preparation of the oral rehydration solution. He discussed this with the staff to confirm his finding. After becoming convinced that there was a need to redesign the sessions and introduce a demonstration on oral rehydration solution preparation, he trained the staff for the same, made the necessary arrangements for logistics, and revised guidelines for conducting awareness-generation sessions.

Communication with Staff

During supervisory rounds or field visits, the manager communicates with different categories of staff members to understand their perceptions of how well they are doing, what problems they face in carrying out their job, what support they need from management to improve their performance, and how better results can be achieved.

Example 3: On a routine round, a hospital manager observed that the pharmacy was crowded and the clients had to spend about 10–15 minutes to buy medicines, which he considered long. He also noticed that some of the clients, who came to the pharmacy with the intent of purchasing medicines, after seeing the queue, changed their mind and returned without making the purchase. The manager interacted with the pharmacists and learned that all the three pharmacists were in position and on the job; there was no vacant position. He interacted with them and learned that they did not face any problem in reading the names of medicines on the prescriptions as most of the doctors prescribed them in legible handwriting. Medicines were stacked systematically on the shelves of the store, and they did not face any problem in locating them. However, the billing process was time consuming and caused delays. The pharmacists requested a separate billing clerk for the pharmacy. But the manager decided to organize training of all the three pharmacists on the billing process. After the training, he authorized them to manage cash.

It should be noted that for many problems, increasing manpower would seem to be a logical solution. But, manpower is an expensive resource, and in many situations, it may not be cost-effective to employ more staff. Additional staff would require additional workstations and logistics to work; the workflow may have to be redesigned. The work load may not be enough throughout the year to keep the additional staff occupied. Therefore, every effort should be made to manage problems with the existing manpower. Strengthening staff members' capacity to improve their skills, strengthening systems or simplifying procedures, involving staff members in multitasking, and encouraging them to increase their efficiency are some of the options.

The manager continued monitoring the billing scenario during his subsequent rounds. Even if a problem is resolved, it may reappear again after some time. Like in this case, as the client load keeps increasing, the waiting time will increase. Thus, monitoring is a continuous process.

Example 4: In a community-based healthcare program, after interacting with the outreach workers, a manager realized that most of their time was spent on commuting to the program areas, and they had much less time for working on the actual interventions. He decided to utilize the services of locally available people even though their capacity was lower.

He made arrangements to strengthen their capacity before inducting them. He revised the recruitment strategy.

Communication with Clients

Informal interactions with clients and their attendants some-times provide valuable insights. In a hospital, such interactions are often possible while clients are waiting to receive certain services or are in the process of leaving the hospital after availing themselves of services.

Example 5: A manager interacted with a patient who was waiting for his turn in the outpatient clinic lounge and learned that the client had been waiting for quite some time even after his appointed time because someone, out of turn, entered the consultant's office. The manager realized that even though the client had not made any formal complaint, he was not happy with the situation. With an increasing client load, such incidents were likely to occur. So, the manager decided to take certain measures to ensure that those arriving first were served first and there was no queue jumping.

Example 6: In a community-based healthcare program, a manager interacted with community members to understand their perspectives. The manager learned that although they get lots of information about family planning methods from out-reach workers, when they visit the local health facilities, they do not regularly get the required family planning commodities or services. Thus, the manager realized that demand-generation interventions were futile without strengthening service delivery.

Review of Records

A manager reviews records of various departments or a pro-gram to assess their operational effectiveness, efficiency, and results.

Example 7: In a hospital, an MRI facility was established. To recover the cost of the machine, the manager determined that the facility needed to conduct a minimum of 10 MRI tests every day to recover the cost of the machine in 3 years. The manager decided to keep track of the use of MRI tests on a day-to-day basis. Whenever there was low utilization, he tried to understand the reason and, if required, took corrective actions.

Example 8: To assess the performance of a community-based healthcare program that aimed to increase the awareness of high-risk groups for HIV/AIDS, the manager can review the number of awareness-generation sessions organized by the program and the number of individuals who attended these sessions. This provides basic information of the number of people contacted by the program staff. It does not provide information about people's awareness of HIV/AIDS or whether their awareness increased as a result of program interventions. For that, we need to measure the awareness of people before and after the sessions. If possible, the relationship between people's awareness of HIV/AIDs and their practices should be studied.

In a community-based healthcare program, if a health worker reports having provided antenatal care to 150 women in 1 year, how do we rate her performance? Absolute numbers have limited value in public health; we need to compare them with something else to reach a conclusion. In certain situations, benchmarks are available for comparison. The number of pregnancies or births happening in a specific area can be determined by multiplying the number of people in that area by the birth rate. For example, if the birth rate in Malawi is 41 per 1000 (population), a village with a population of 1000 is expected to have 41 women becoming pregnant every year, and 41 births (excluding abortions). If a health worker covers a population of 5000, she can expect about 200 pregnant women every year, and if she provided antenatal coverage to 150 women, it gives the impression that she might have missed out some of the pregnant women.

Family planning programs generally work with people of reproductive age, known as eligible couples. A census or district-level health surveys or national family health surveys can provide information on the number of eligible couples in a community. For example, in rural India, eligible couples constitute about 16% of the population. That means, that in a village with a population of 1000 people, about 160 couples might be expected to need family planning services. Thus, we can assess the performance of an outreach worker by comparing her performance against such benchmarks.

Managing Problems

When there are many problems and it is often not possible for a manager to resolve all of them, a logical option is to prioritize.

Prioritization

In a hospital or healthcare setting, the following criteria can be used for prioritization:

1. Issues that endanger the safety of the clients
2. Issues that result in poor clinical outcomes
3. Issues that causes dissatisfaction among clients

Client safety is paramount and has to be the top priority of all in healthcare organizations. For example, the presence of an incompetent surgeon in a hospital is a serious risk to the safety of clients and should be dealt with as a top priority. Postoperative infections adversely affect clinical outcomes and, therefore, need immediate corrective actions. Delays in providing services to client or inappropriate behavior by staff would invariably result in client dissatisfaction and need to be addressed.

Root-Cause Analysis

To devise appropriate corrective actions, the root cause of the problem needs to be understood. For example, if the process of registration takes longer than expected, the manager needs to identify the reason. Some of the reasons could be

1. Complicated registration forms or poorly designed computer programs or cumbersome procedures
2. Shortage of currency denominations and staff facing problems with managing cash and returning any balance to clients
3. Problems with the printer, delay in getting printouts
4. Small space causing chaos or confusion
5. Inadequate number of staff resulting in overcrowding at the registration desk
6. Poor computer skills of staff
7. Poor motivation of the staff to dispose of the clients quickly

Initially, the manager should focus on issues that are related to the hospital system (numbers 1–5 in the previous list). After that, if the problem persists, he may scrutinize the performance of individual staff members (numbers 6 and 7), and take corrective actions, if required.

Information Needs of Top Management

Organizations generally produce lots of data, not all of which may be relevant for its top management. Top management can be more effective if it receives selective data or information, based on which they can make decisions. The top management of a service organization needs to know about the quality of services provided, and the effectiveness and efficiency of its operations. The information needs of top management in a hospital setting and in a community-based health program are explained separately.

Information Needs in a Hospital Setting

In a hospital setting, top management requires information on

■ Patient safety
■ Financial returns
■ Utilization of services
■ Efficiency of certain services
■ Performance of a new initiative, if any

Patient safety: Any unnatural death, accident, serious adverse reactions to medicines or blood transfusions, major complications, or hospital-acquired infections, if any, needs top management's attention as a top priority.

Financial returns: A hospital gets maximum profit from the following centers:

1. Operation theaters
2. Laboratories
3. Radiology
4. Pharmacy
5. Intensive care units

It is important for the top management of a hospital to keep a close watch on the revenue returns from these departments on a day-to-day basis. Figures of the previous year can be used as benchmarks and projections can be made by adding a growth factor of about 10–20% over these. For example, if daily sales in the pharmacy during the previous year was 100,000 rupees. By adding a growth factor of 15%, we may expect the daily sales during the current year to be 115,000 rupees. Keeping in view day-to-day variations, a normal range can be worked out, say 100,000 to 130,000 rupees.

Software programs can be designed to raise a red flag in case sales drop below 100,000 rupees. During festivals, hospital business is expected to go down and that needs to be taken into account.

Utilization of services: The revenue income of the hospital is dependent on the utilization of services. So, indirectly, income indicates the utilization. Still it may be useful for top management to track service statistics, such as

- Daily outpatient attendance
- Bed occupancy rate in the wards

Trends in the two previously mentioned indicators can be helpful for management when they make plans for the future.

- Number of high-end surgeries—cardiac bypass grafting, organ transplants, joint replacements, and so on
- Number of high-end diagnostic tests like MRI tests, CT scans, angiographies, and so on

Information on the above indicators can give some idea of the current trends in clinical practices and may give some indication of possibilities of malpractice by some professionals.

Efficiency of services: This is mostly measured in terms of cost incurred in providing a certain amount of a service. However, certain indicators in a hospital show efficiency without going into the financials. The average length of stay of patients in various wards is an indicator of efficiency of indoor services. Similarly, turnaround time between surgeries is a measure of efficiency of surgical services.

Performance of new initiatives: If a new department is set up or a new activity started, top management may like to review its performance closely by keeping track of footfall, the number of procedures done, revenue income, and client satisfaction.

Information Needs of a Community-Based Healthcare Program

Community-based healthcare programs have a specific agenda and objectives, based on which they define their key result areas (KRAs). Accordingly, the top management of the organization may like to monitor progress or achievements of KRAs. For example, in the case of an organization providing family planning services to the community, top management may like to track the following statistics:

1. Number of clients served—for each type of service they provide: tubal ligation, no-scalpel vasectomy, intrauterine contraceptive device insertion, hormonal implant, or contraceptive injections.
2. Number of complications, failures, or deaths, particularly from surgical procedures.
3. Unit cost of providing each service.

Similarly, in a healthcare organization working on capacity building of healthcare service providers, the following may be monitored:

1. Number of service providers trained on specific clinical skills
2. Number of clients served or procedures done by the trained providers—comparison of pre- and post-training performance of each provider
3. Number of complications, failures, or deaths caused by the trained providers—pre- and post-training comparison
4. Client satisfaction—pre- and post-training comparison
5. Cost of training a service provider

Chapter 12

Evaluation

The process of judging the value of an institution or a program by systematic measurement is known as evaluation. We can evaluate the quality of services offered by a hospital. We can measure the effectiveness and efficiency of its operations; we can determine whether the profit earned by the hospital is worth the investment made on its establishment. We can also determine whether the hospital is fulfilling its mission and practicing the values it envisaged. We can even attempt to study whether the hospital is making an impact on the health and well-being of the people in the community it serves. Similarly, a community-based healthcare project can be evaluated to determine if it is achieving its objectives.

While institutions and long-term programs can be evaluated at any stage, time-bound projects are generally evaluated either mid-term or toward the end of the project period. An evaluation study can recommend continuing the program in its present form or can suggest revising its approach, priorities, or strategies; it may recommend reallocation of resources. If an evaluation study finds that the program is not fulfilling its objectives, it may recommend its closure. To avoid the possibilities of bias, an external agency is generally asked to conduct the evaluation.

"Monitoring and evaluation" is sometimes used as a single term, for example, department of monitoring and evaluation or manager of monitoring and evaluation. Both "monitoring" and "evaluation" aim toward improving the situation by identifying gaps, if any, in implementation; however, the difference between the two terms should be clearly understood. Monitoring is a continuous, ongoing process during the process of implementation, while evaluation is one-time activity. Monitoring is done by the supervisors who implement the program, whereas, evaluation is done by an external agency. Monitoring aims to identify challenges or gaps in executing planned activities and to find quick practical solutions, whereas, an evaluation may suggest wholesale changes.

Scope of Evaluation

An entire organization or project can be evaluated or evaluation can be limited to a specific department, activity, service, or staff. For example, an evaluation assessed the utility of the maintenance department of a hospital and determined whether contracting out maintenance services would be a more cost-effective option. An evaluation study can be focused on a specific category of staff; for example, an evaluation measuring the clinical and interpersonal skills of nurses in a hospital.

An evaluation study can be quantitative, qualitative, or a mix of both. For example, a hospital established a high-tech physiotherapy unit at a huge cost. After one year, it would be prudent to evaluate its utilization. This study would be predominantly quantitative, determining the number of clients who utilized the service in the last year and the income from this. It will examine the capital and recurring expenses of the facility. It can determine when the facility is likely to reach the break-even stage. The study may also incorporate a qualitative component of assessing client satisfaction. It may also assess the perception of other relevant departments, such as the orthopedic department, intensive care units, or chronic care wards, which mostly require physiotherapy services for their clients. An evaluation of satisfaction of the front office staff would be predominantly a qualitative study enumerating the reasons for their satisfaction or dissatisfaction.

Systems Framework

The quality framework or systems framework suggested by Avedis Donabedian delineated the three major components of an organization:

■ Structure—building, manpower, equipment and materials, rules and regulations
■ Process—clinical and non-clinical processes
■ Output—number of people treated and patient satisfaction

Structure leads to processes, and the processes lead to output. Output, in the long term leads to outcome. And the outcome, in a still longer term, leads to impact, as shown subsequently:

The components of this trail may overlap in some situations. *Example*: A hospital provides knee replacement surgeries. The surgeons and support staff, operating theater, instruments, and so on, constitute the "structure" of the knee replacement services. The surgical procedures, interpersonal communication by the service providers, and managerial activities in the department are the "processes." The number of patients treated with knee replacements during a specific period is the "output"

of this program. The number of years the treated clients can walk normally after the surgery can be considered the program's "outcome." The proportion of them leading an economically productive life after the surgery, and for how many years, indicates the "impact" of the knee replacement program. Impact of a program also refers to its long-term benefits on the socio-economic status of a community. Systems framework is further explained in Chapter 6, "Quality Improvement."

An evaluation study can limit itself to studying the structure, processes, or output. It can also attempt to study the outcome and even impact. For obvious reasons, assessing the impact of a program can be challenging. It is necessary to define the scope of evaluation: What exactly will be studied or measured.

Method of Evaluation

Evaluation is a kind of research study and involves the methods used in research studies.

Study Question

An evaluation begins with one or more study questions. Here are some examples of study questions:

- What is the quality of family planning services provided by public health systems in a particular district?
- How satisfied are security staff members in a particular hospital? What problems do they face in carrying out their job? How can their working conditions be improved?

Study Population

The people who are likely to provide useful information in answering the study questions constitute the study population. For example, in the previous example of evaluation of security staff satisfaction, the people who may provide some useful information would be the security staff members themselves, their supervisors, hospital staff, and visitors of patients. If the study population is large, a sample from it can be drawn systematically.

Data Collection Techniques

To answer the study questions, investigators collect information from the study population. They can employ the following methods for collecting the information:

■ Interviewing key informants from the study population.
■ Observing the upkeep of the facility and maintenance of equipment; observing whether the clinical procedures conform to clinical protocols and guidelines.
■ Reviewing records, such as service statistics, patient bills, and report of death audit.

Data Collection Tools

To ensure consistency of the information collected by an investigator from various respondents or information collected by many investigators, certain tools are used for data collection. The tools are known as study tools or study instruments. They could be

■ Questionnaires
■ Checklists

Questionnaires: Investigators conduct interviews with the help of questionnaires. Each study question is broken down into several questions. They all constitute a questionnaire. A questionnaire can have as many questions as can be answered comfortably by a respondent in one session. The questions can be close-ended, open-ended, or a mix of both. A close-ended question has one correct answer out of several options.

For example, how many times were the reports of a histopathology examination found incorrect during the last month? The options are: 0–5, 6–10, 11–15, or, 16 or more. An example of an open-ended question is: How do you perceive the quality of services in this health center?

Checklists: Observations are made or records are studied with the help of checklists. A checklist may not have specific questions but rather a list of issues for which information is needed. As an example, a checklist used for observing a laboratory included the following issues:

■ Availability of laboratory technicians and technologists— their qualification and experience
■ Equipment—available equipment, level of automation, system for maintenance and upkeep
■ Adequacy of reagents and supplies, and system for replenishment
■ Arrangement for uninterrupted electricity and water supply
■ Cleanliness and upkeep of the premises
■ Availability of protocols and standard operating procedures (SOPs) for various procedures
■ System for internal and external quality checks
■ Accreditation with the National Accreditation Board for Laboratories (NABL)
■ Utilization of laboratory services
■ Utilization of high-end or expensive diagnostic tests
■ Proportion of samples that could not be tested due to inadequate sample or clotting of blood
■ Average time required to report common emergency tests

Data Collection

Trained investigators interview the selected key informants (also known as respondents) and fill in the questionnaires. Similarly, they record their findings from observations or through review of records.

Data Analysis and Report Writing

Collected data is analyzed to answer the study questions. In quantitative studies, the findings are generally presented in percentages. For example, in the evaluation of a laboratory, the findings may be: All the laboratory technicians were skilled in performing common investigations. Only 3% of the samples could not be tested because the blood samples were clotted. For emergency reports, 80% were provided within one hour of submitting the samples.

In the case of a community-based quantitative evaluation, the findings could be something like: 67% of adolescent girls were aware of safe-sex practices, whereas only 59% boys were aware of the same.

Qualitative evaluations generally do not quantify the findings and speak about a majority. For example, an evaluation study of satisfaction among security staff may come out with a finding that the majority of the security staff of the hospital is dissatisfied with working conditions. Security staff members face problems in confronting patients' visitors, particularly those who push them to make their way to wards, and they feel helpless in taking any action against them. They may be unhappy that they have to stand for long hours, or they do not get relief to have a tea break. Similarly, in a community-based healthcare program, if the study is aimed at assessing the interpersonal skills of outreach workers, it should conclude if the interpersonal skills of the majority of the workers are good, satisfactory, or poor. Whether they are able to influence behavior change among the target population? Anecdotes can provide insight into the situation.

In the end, evaluation studies generally make recommendations for improving the situation. The recommendations have to come from the study findings. In the previous example of outreach workers, the study may further recommend what could be done to improve their interpersonal skills. The study may also identify the workers who have exceptionally good interpersonal skills and who could be utilized for training their peers.

Examples of Evaluation Studies

Example 1: Evaluation of Emergency Services in a Hospital

The study attempted to answer the following questions:

Structure

- Infrastructure: Is the space provided to the emergency room adequate?
- Manpower: Are the human resources: medical officers, nurses, and support staff adequate in each shift? Are they trained and competent to handle emergency cases?
- Equipment and materials: Is the equipment for resuscitation, the crash cart, in working condition, and are emergency medicines available?
- Clinical protocols: Are clinical protocols for managing common emergencies defined and known to the service providers?
- Specialized care: Does the emergency department have linkages with specialists?
- Investigation facilities: Does the emergency department have the facilities for conducting required investigations?

Process

- Are the patients who utilize the services really in actual emergency? What proportion of cases are in a life-threatening condition?
- How promptly do doctors or nurses attend to the emergency cases?
- What proportion of cases require specialists' attention?
- How much time do specialists generally take to attend to an emergency case?
- Are clinical protocols and guidelines being followed?

- What proportion of cases needs investigations, admission, and surgery?
- Is there a problem in admitting emergency cases in intensive care units due to a shortage of beds?
- Are there delays in starting surgery in emergency cases?
- How many cases are brought in dead?
- How many medico-legal cases are attended to?

Output

- What is the utilization of emergency services during different shifts?
- What proportion of cases are referred to higher hospitals?
- How many deaths occur during the course of treatment?
- What is the utilization of ambulances?
- How satisfied are the clients? How satisfied are the service providers?
- What is the profit or loss to the hospital from emergency services?

Example 2: Evaluation of Community-Based Diarrhea Control Program

The study attempted to provide information on the following themes:

Structure

- Coverage of the program in terms of geography and population
- Program team size
- Competence of field workers in conducting awareness or education sessions; their motivation
- Coverage provided by one field worker—geographical and thematic

- Mobility of the field workers
- Mechanism for supervision of field workers
- Reporting system

Processes

- Number of awareness or education sessions held by program staff with community members
- Number of mothers/caregivers contacted and provided with information on prevention and management of diarrhea
- Number of children identified as having diarrhea and provided with ORS and zinc

Output

Number of children treated for diarrhea with ORS and zinc.

Outcome

Reduction in childhood malnutrition.

Impact

Reduction in childhood mortality due to diarrhea in the project area after the program intervention.

Bibliography

Avedis Donabedian, *An Introduction to Quality Assurance in Health Care*, Oxfrod University Press, 2003.
Rosemary McMahon et al., *On Being in Charge*, WHO, 1992.

Chapter 13

Medical Audit

The official verification of accounts of transactions is known as an audit. Finance and accounting professionals conduct audits to verify whether the financial transactions made in an organization were in compliance with laid out procedures; whether funds or amounts received were properly accounted for; and whether payments made to the staff or vendors or purchases made were duly approved by a competent authority.

In hospitals, besides a financial audit, a medical audit can be conducted to examine the quality of clinical care. A medical audit involves the retrospective review of clinical records to identify gaps, if any, in providing clinical care. The purpose of the medical audit is to improve the quality of clinical care by filling the identified gaps. There is no intention to identify the professionals who made mistakes; their names are not recorded or disclosed. The terms "medical audit" and "clinical audit" are used interchangeably.

A medical audit can be conducted for

- A specific disease or condition
- A specific procedure or surgery
- An unnatural event, unexpected result, or interesting finding
- A death—this is also known as a death audit

Medical audits generally attempt to answer the following questions:

- Whether the patient was attended to promptly?
- Was the diagnosis correct?
- Whether the treatment given was appropriate and in conformance with clinical protocols?
- Was there any negligence in administering the treatment?
- Was the outcome of the treatment satisfactory?
- Was there anything else that could have been done to reach a better outcome.

The availability of well-maintained patient records is a prerequisite for medical audits. If the initiative to start the process of medical audits in a hospital comes from medical professionals, the outcomes are likely to be better.

Steps in a Medical Audit

A typical medical audit involves the following steps:

Constitution of a Medical Audit Committee

A medical audit committee should be constituted in each major clinical department of a hospital, comprising of 2–3 clinicians. They may be from the same specialty or related disciplines. The committee should assemble periodically, say, every quarter to conduct medical audits. The members of the committee may change periodically.

Selection of a Disease/Condition

The audit committee selects a disease, diagnosis, or condition for conducting a medical audit. If there were complaints or cases of client dissatisfaction for a particular disease or condition, this represents an opportunity to conduct a medical audit for that condition. An adverse outcome of a treatment or Anything of interest to medical professionals can also be audited. If there is no reason for a medical audit, the subject of the medical audit may be selected randomly.

Developing a Checklist

The audit committee develops criteria for assessing the quality of care of the selected disease or condition. For example, to audit dengue fever cases, the following criteria were developed:

- Whether an appropriate blood test was carried out to diagnose dengue—PCR or NS1 by ELISA
- Whether patients' vital signs, such as blood pressure, pulse, temperature, respiratory rate, and blood volume were monitored regularly
- Whether the optimal blood volume was maintained by administering ringer lactate, colloids, or blood products
- Whether signs of complications, such as hemorrhage, pneumonia, bone marrow failure, hepatitis, iritis, or retinal hemorrhage were monitored
- Whether unnecessary injections, antibiotics, or analgesics such as aspirin or ibuprofen were avoided

Selection of Patient Files

A reference period is specified. For example, the committee may decide to conduct an audit of a specific condition that was treated in the hospital during the last 3 months.

From the medical records department, all the patient files of the selected disease are taken out for that specified period. If their number is very large, a smaller sample can be drawn. For example, every second or third case can be selected from the patient files that are arranged chronologically. When a sample is used, the sampling methods and sampling intervals should be specified.

Examination of Selected Patient Files

The audit committee examines each patient file against the predetermined criteria of the checklist. They record their findings on a worksheet (see Table 13.1) and award marks, say, "1" for a positive finding or when the criterion is fulfilled, and "0" for a negative finding or when the criterion is not fulfilled.

Analysis of Data and Report Writing

The collected data is analyzed and a brief report is prepared enumerating salient positive and negative findings. Wherever possible, a comparison is made with national or international standards.

Sharing of Findings and Corrective Actions

A meeting of all the clinicians of the department is called, wherein medical audit committee members make a presentation of the salient findings of their audit. The names of the treating clinicians are not shared. No efforts are made to fix responsibilities for the identified gaps. This is followed by an open discussion, and the doctors are encouraged to state how they would like to prevent the identified mistakes in the future; what they would like to do differently. The outcome of the meeting is recorded and circulated to all the doctors of the department.

If an action is required on the part of nurses, technicians, or others, relevant information is shared with them separately.

Review Audit

After a span of about 3 to 6 months, a repeat audit is carried out to check if the situation has improved.

Examples

Example 1: Medical Audit of Malaria Cases

The criteria developed by a medical audit committee to examine malaria cases are given in the worksheet. The worksheet presents data from four patient files: (Table 13.1)

Table 13.1   Medical Audit Worksheet

S.N.	Criteria for Malaria Cases—Desired Standard	Patient Files				
		1	2	3	4	Total
1	Time lag between admission of patient and collection of blood smear—less than 1 hour	1	0	1	0	2
2	Other similar conditions ruled out by appropriate investigations—Yes	1	1	1	1	4
3	Time interval between the blood smear collected and report available—less than 6 hours	1	1	1	1	4
4	Time interval between the blood smear report available and prescription of antimalarial medicines—less than 1 hour	1	1	1	1	4
5	Appropriateness of antimalarial medicines as per blood report—Artemisinin-based combination therapy (ACT)	1	1	1	0	3
6	Six hourly recordings of patient vitals: Temperature, pulse, blood pressure, and respiratory rate—Yes	1	0	1	0	2
7	Administration of complete course of antimalarial medicines—Yes	1	0	0	0	1
8	Unnecessary antibiotics administered—No	1	1	1	0	3

Note: Mark 1 is given when the criterion is fulfilled, and 0 is given when it is not fulfilled.

Analysis of the data from four patient files of the previously mentioned worksheet revealed the following:

Positive Findings

1. Other similar conditions were ruled out by appropriate diagnostic tests in all the cases
2. There were no delays in providing the blood smear reports
3. There were no delays in prescribing appropriate antimalarial medicines

Negative Findings

1. There were delays in collecting blood smear in half of the cases
2. The prescribed antimalarial medicine was not appropriate in 25% of cases
3. Monitoring of vital signs was lacking in 50% of cases
4. Complete course of treatment was not administered to 75% of cases
5. Unnecessary antibiotics were advised in 25% of cases

After analyzing the data, the audit team shared the findings with all clinicians in a meeting. During open discussions, they all agreed to adhere to the clinical protocol for prescribing the correct antimalarial medicines. Some of them also agreed that they would not prescribe any antibiotic without a specific reason. The pathologist agreed to set up a system for collecting samples for diagnostics tests from the admitted patients as soon as possible after the consultants' advice. He assured of regular monitoring to ensure prompt laboratory services to the admitted patients. The ward in charge agreed to speak to the nurse in charge to ensure the meticulous recording of vital signs of all patients.

Example 3: Medical Audit for Head Injury Cases

Criteria:

- Whether the vital signs of the patient were monitored continuously
- Whether a CT scan was done urgently, and time lag if any
- If intracranial pressure was raised, whether corrective actions were taken, such as intravenous mannitol, CSF drainage, and hyperventilation
- If the facility was not appropriate for managing head injury cases, whether timely referred was made to a higher center after stabilizing the patient

Example 4: Medical Audit of Coronary Heart Disease (Heart Attack)

Criteria:

- On suspicion of heart attack, whether sublingual nitroglycerin was administered immediately (if not contraindicated)
- Whether ECG test was taken urgently? Time lag if any
- On confirmation of myocardial infarction, prompt percutaneous coronary intervention (PCI) or thrombolytic therapy was administered, time lag if any
- Whether vital signs, particularly blood pressure were monitored and maintained

Example 5: Death Audit

A patient reported to the emergency room of a hospital with complaints of acute severe pain in the abdomen. He was kept under observation and given some treatment, but he died after a few hours. A death audit was carried out and the audit committee made the following observations:

- There was a history of a fight between the deceased and another person; the service provider did not record this important finding and did not give it due importance while managing the case.
- Ultrasonography of the abdomen should have been advised immediately, which was not done. Instead, an X-ray of the abdomen was taken, but its report was not collected until the patient died.
- Examination findings including vital signs were recorded appropriately at the time of admission of the patient. The patient's vital signs were normal at the time of admission. Appropriate intravenous fluids and antispasmodic medicine were administered. Oral food and fluids were appropriately stopped.
- It was found that the patient's vitals were stable for about an hour after the admission but thereafter they started deteriorating, possibly due to an internal hemorrhage. But, the attending doctors and nurses did not take cognizance of this development and did not take any remedial action.
- The medical audit concluded that it was a case of medical negligence, and death could have been averted by promptly identifying the deterioration in the patient's vitals due to internal hemorrhage and by carrying out urgent surgery.

Medical Audit of Surgical Cases

If there are indications that unnecessary surgical procedures, such as hysterectomies or appendectomies, are carried out by some surgeons in a hospital, a medical audit can find out the proportion of cases in which histopathological reports of the removed tissues were normal. A guideline will have to be framed that whenever an organ is removed during surgical procedures, the removed tissues will be subjected to histopathological examination.

Medical Audit of Unnatural Event or Unexpected Results

In cases of unnatural events, unexpected results, or interesting findings, medical audits can be conducted to develop a better understanding of the cases.

Medical audits, if carried out in the right spirit, can bring about phenomenal improvements in the quality of clinical care.

Chapter 14

Healthcare Systems

The healthcare system is comprised of a set of interconnected healthcare facilities with service providers aiming to provide healthcare services to communities and improve their health status. It includes a mechanism for governance and management for these facilities. There are two broad dimensions of healthcare:

- Hospital-based care
- Public health or community-based care

Hospital-Based Care

When people fall sick or sustain injuries, they generally avail of services from a medical practitioner, clinic, or hospital. The care or services provided by these establishments are mostly curative services and are known as medical care or medical services.

Community-Based Care

Besides curative services, people also need to be protected from certain diseases or injuries. For example, children are to be protected from diseases like poliomyelitis, measles, diphtheria, whooping cough, tetanus, hepatitis B, influenza, and so on, through immunization. Women need to be protected during pregnancy and childbirth. They need to be provided with antenatal care, safe delivery services, and postnatal care. Many children in economically weaker communities are malnourished and stunted. They need supplementary nutrition and growth monitoring. Many children require treatment for intestinal worms. There may be people in the community suffering from diseases, such as tuberculosis, leprosy, or HIV/AIDS, and they may be ignorant about it. Some of them may pose a risk to others. There can be endemic diseases like malaria or dengue fever affecting a large number of people. Many of these problems require interventions at the community level. Efforts to improve the healthstatus of a community with the participation of its people are known as "public health" or "community-based systems."

If certain health problems cannot be managed at a community-level the clients can be referred to higher-level facilities or hospitals. For example, premature or low-birthweight babies may require care in the neonatal intensive care unit of a specialized hospital. Similarly, advanced cases of tuberculosis, leprosy, or AIDS may require treatment in a hospital. Thus, the community-based system needs to be linked to hospitals through a referral system.

Ownership of Healthcare Services

In many countries, governments establish and own most healthcare services, both hospital-based and community-based. In some countries, private organizations including corporate hospitals, charitable organizations, nongovernmental organizations (NGOs), and civil society supplement the efforts of government.

Public Health System

A public health system or government-owned system comprises both hospitals and the public health system. Through its network of health centers and hospitals it provides healthcare services to the masses, particularly in rural and remote areas. Although every country has a different structure, the general concept of a public health system is explained subsequently.

Health subcenter: The most peripheral service delivery unit is commonly known as a health subcenter or health post. These centers are generally managed by a lone service provider, who may be a nurse, paramedic, or health worker. The center provides coverage to a defined population, say 5000 people living in 5–10 villages. These centers are generally accommodated in a small house having 1–2 rooms and a waiting area. A water supply and toilet may be available in some places. Healthcare services that can be provided through these centers include immunization of children, antenatal and postnatal care, supply of family planning commodities, directly observed treatment (DOTS) of tuberculosis, presumptive treatment of malaria, and treatment of common ailments like diarrhea and acute respiratory infections in children. In some countries, there is a provision to conduct deliveries in these centers. In that case, a trained midwife, a room with a labor table, water supply, and a toilet are needed.

If community members do not visit the health centers, it is the responsibility of the health worker to reach out to them in their homes. This concept is known as "outreach." The health worker of a subcenter is expected to visit each village in her catchment area on a fixed day of the week. During her visit to the village, she is expected to contact specific groups. She is required to contact eligible couples and educate them on family planning; newlywed couples are educated to delay their first child and others are educated to keep a gap of three years between two children (spacing). The health worker can provide them with common family planning commodities like oral contraceptive pills or condoms. Couples who have completed their families are counseled on long-acting methods, such as implant or intrauterine contraceptive device or permanent methods, such as a sterilization procedure. The health worker facilitates interested clients to avail of services in higher-level facilities.

The health worker identifies women in the village who have conceived. She registers pregnant women, if any, and organizes the provision of antenatal care. When a woman approaches delivery, she educates her on a safe delivery and facilitates her visit to an institution to deliver there.

After a child is born, the health worker keeps track of the child's milestones, arranges to provide immunization and support in growth monitoring.

Health workers also contact adolescent girls and educate them on menstrual hygiene and on prevention of anemia, which are common problems with adolescent girls in poor communities. She also guides them on preventing unwanted pregnancies and protecting themselves from HIV and other sexually transmitted infections.

In economically developed communities, health workers may contact elderly or geriatric people and help them in tackling health problems. Thus, healthcare services are provided at every important stage of life, and this concept is known as the "life-cycle approach."

About six such health subcenters are linked to higher centers known as primary health centers. When the service provider of a health subcenter is not able to manage the problems of a client, the client is referred to the primary health center. For example, if a child with diarrhea develops dehydration and requires intravenous fluids, which are not available in the subcenter, the child can be referred to a primary health center.

Primary health center: A primary health center caters to a larger population, about 30,000 people. It is generally headed by a medical officer, who is a family physician or a general doctor.

Primary health centers can have about 8–10 staff members including a nurse, pharmacist, laboratory technician, extension educator, housekeeping person, and male and female outreach workers. The medical officer also supervises the nurses or paramedical workers of the attached health subcenters. The primary health center is usually housed in a building with 8–10 rooms. It has a pharmacy, a laboratory, a delivery room, a procedure room, and a waiting area. There can be a few indoor beds to keep clients under observation for a few hours. Most of these centers do not have the facilities or staff, particularly nurses, to manage clients overnight. The laboratory generally has facilities to diagnose anemia, pregnancy, malaria, tuberculosis, and so on.

A primary health center provides services such as antenatal care, normal deliveries, postnatal care, immunization, treatment of common ailments such as malaria, tuberculosis, dengue fever, injuries, and so on. Complicated cases that require specialized care can be referred to higher centers.

The primary health center, along with its set of subcenters, provides the first level of healthcare services known as "primary level of care." The thrust of the services is on preventive and promotive care. In addition, they provide treatment of common ailments.

District hospital: At the district level, district hospitals provide a secondary level of care. The population size of a district can vary widely between countries; it may be up to 3 million people. They provide specialized care and all have broad specialties, such as medicine, surgery, gynecology-obstetrics, anesthesia, ophthalmology, ear-nose-throat (ENT), dermatology, psychiatry, pathology, and radiology. The hospitals have full-fledged operating rooms and can conduct caesarean sections and general surgeries. There is provision for newborn care and neonatal intensive care facility. They have a pathology laboratory, X-ray, and ultrasonography facilities. They also have a specialized tuberculosis clinic for diagnosis and treatment of tuberculosis cases, including complicated cases. Diagnosis of medical problems like malaria, typhoid, dengue, or pneumonia, by proper diagnostic tests, and their treatment is possible in district hospitals. Facilities for male and female sterilization surgeries and cataract surgeries are generally available. There are facilities for HIV testing and counseling. Antiretroviral treatment for HIV may not be available in all district hospitals. District hospitals generally have inpatient facilities with 50–100 beds and round-the-clock nursing care. They can attend to emergencies round the clock. A district hospital can have 15–20 doctors including 10 specialists and a total strength of about 100 staff members. For advanced or complicated cases, or if there is a requirement for super-specialty care, such as cardiology or neurology, they can refer the clients to higher-level hospitals, which are super-specialty hospitals or teaching hospitals. Such hospitals are generally located in cities.

Subdistrict hospitals: To bridge the gap between a primary health center and a district hospital, in some countries, an intermediate level of hospitals, known as subdistrict hospitals, are set up between the two. The subdistrict hospitals, in addition to the facilities of a primary health center, provide emergency obstetric care and newborn care. They should have facilities to conduct deliveries, cesarean sections, and manage premature or low-birthweight babies. Accordingly, subdistrict hospitals should have a few specialities: gynecology-obstetrics, pediatrics, surgery, and anesthesia, in addition to a few general doctors. These hospitals can cover a population of about 100,000.

Hospitals in cities: In cities, local municipal committees, provincial governments, or national governments set up hospitals. They can be single-specialty or multispecialty hospitals; they can also be teaching hospitals.

Village-Level Volunteers

A shortage of trained manpower in the health sector, particularly in rural and remote areas is a major challenge in many countries. Many sanctioned positions in public health systems remain vacant either because of the nonavailability of the right candidates and because of the ineffectiveness of the system in recruiting personnel. To overcome this challenge, a novel experiment was done by the Indian government. It created a band of village-level volunteers known as accredited social health activists (ASHA). From each village, one young woman with a minimum qualification of a 10th standard, who volunteers to provide healthcare services to the village population, is identified and trained by the public health system. Each ASHA is attached to a specific health center and provides services in her village. They help in demand generation and they facilitate women and children to avail of healthcare services. They identify pregnant women in their village and encourage them to avail of antenatal care and facilitate their availing of an institutional delivery. In return, they receive a nominal honorarium. As a result of their interventions, there is a sharp increase in uptake of institutional deliveries. They facilitate routine immunization of children and promote use of contraceptives.

Private Health Sector

In the private sector, medical care is provided by a variety of players. They can be single practitioner clinics, who may be qualified or unqualified, practitioners of other systems of medicine, such as Ayurveda, homeopathy, acupuncture, and so on. There are hospitals in the private sector, which can be small, medium, or large. They may be single-specialty or multispecialty. There are also super-specialty hospitals or teaching hospitals.

In some places, charitable organizations and NGOs supplement the efforts of the public health system in providing community-based services. Organizations that work on health issues at the community level are known as healthcare organizations.

Healthcare is a broader domain encompassing hospital-based medical care and public health or community-based care. Public health and hospital-based services complement one another. The management of hospitals or clinics is known as hospital management. Management of community-based health programs is known as health management or health-care management.

Community-Based Programs

NGOs or community-based healthcare organizations generally work on specific health issues, such as

- *Family planning services*: Marie Stopes, India organizes family planning camps in public health facilities in remote and hard-to-reach areas and offers tubal ligation, IUCD insertion, and vasectomy services to eligible clients.
- *Tuberculosis*: The International Union against Tuberculosis and Lung Diseases (IUTLD) provides technical support to governments and NGOs in the prevention and treatment of tuberculosis.
- *Diarrhea*: FHI 360, an international NGO worked on the social marketing of oral rehydration salt and zinc for treatment of diarrhea in children.
- *HIV/AIDS*: The International HIV/AIDS Alliance works to provide care and support to people living with HIV/AIDS.
- *Leprosy*: Leprosy Mission works on the prevention and treatment of leprosy.
- Some organizations provide mobile clinics in hard-to-reach areas or provide emergency ambulance services.

Some NGOs work on broader areas, such as

- *Awareness generation*: Some NGOs work to increasing awareness among people in underserved areas on specific health issues. They provide information to dispel misconceptions or try to change their behavior or practices. For example, in some communities, newborn babies are given a bath immediately after the birth, which can expose them to hypothermia, particularly in cold weather. Hypothermia is an important cause of infant deaths. Project Concern International worked on educating women in Bihar, India to not bathe their newborn babies for one week after birth.

Similarly, Path Finder International works to increase awareness among adolescent girls on safe sexual and reproductive health.

■ *Social marketing*: Some organizations use commercial marketing techniques to promote certain healthy practices in a community. Population Services International (PSI), an NGO, works to promote the use of condoms and IUCDs in certain areas.

■ *Capacity building*: Some healthcare organizations work to strengthen the capacity of community-based healthcare service providers. EngenderHealth, an international NGO, conducts training of doctors in tubal ligation or no-scalpel vasectomy services, and in improving the quality of family planning services.

Jhpiego, and international NGO, conducts training of nurses in IUCD insertion and removal. It also works to strengthen preservice education of nurses.

Similarly, Ipas, an international NGO, conducts training for service providers on manual vacuum aspiration (MVA), which is a safe procedure for abortion.

■ *Research*: Some healthcare organizations, like the Indian Institute of Health Management Research (IIHMR) and the Foundation of Research in Health Systems (FRHS), conduct research to understand the magnitude of a health problem in a community or determine its root cause. They measure the effectiveness of health programs or evaluate their impact.

Chapter 15

Infection Prevention

Many hospital and healthcare managers may wonder whether "infection prevention" is their domain. Well, prevention as well as treatment of infections in individual patients is the responsibility of their treating doctors, nurses, and other clinical staff. But, setting up a system for infection prevention in a hospital and its monitoring is the responsibility of a manager. Hospital and healthcare managers, even if nonmedical, need to be aware of the basics of infection prevention.

Hospitals contribute a great deal to managing infections in individual patients, but they are also a source of infections. New infections acquired by people during their stay in a hospital are known as hospital-acquired infections, if these infections were neither present nor incubating at the time of contact. It is not only patients and their family members who visit them that can catch hospital-acquired infections, the hospital staff also sometimes acquires them.

Hospital-acquired infections add to the suffering of patients; their stay in the hospital gets extended and the cost of care escalates. Some patients even die from these infections. Globally, hospital-acquired infections are a matter of serious concern and a big challenge.

If a patient undergoing treatment develops a new infection, sometimes the treating physicians treats the infection straight-away rather than taking the trouble to investigate the source of infection, causative agent, and its mode of transmission, before starting treatment. As a result, many hospital-acquired infections remain unrecorded and unreported.

Types of Hospital-Acquired Infections

The following types of hospital-acquired infections are common:

■ Urinary tract infections
■ Surgical site infections
■ Respiratory tract infections
■ Blood infections

Urinary Tract Infections

Urinary tract infections (UTI) are usually caused by catheter-ization. Patients who are critically ill and have no control over their bladder, patients who undergo major surgeries under general anesthesia, and patients with obstructive lesions in their urinary passage are often catheterized, and many develop infections. These infections can occur despite service providers taking all precautions. During the process of cath-eterization, the commensal organisms in the distal part of the urethra get pushed inside the urethra along with the catheter. There they find favorable conditions; they multiply, and grow, resulting in infection. UTIs often present with symptoms of a fever and a burning sensation during micturition.

Surgical Site Infections

Some of the postoperative patients develop surgical site infections (SSIs). These infections are commonly acquired during surgical procedures when the tissues are cut open and exposed to the environment. Direct contact is the most common mode of transmission of surgical site infections. Contaminated surgical instruments, gauze pieces, and gloved hands are common sources of infections. Dust particles or human droplets can also fall on the exposed tissues and cause infection. Organisms get trapped inside the tissues when the overlying skin is closed on completion of the procedure, they find the conditions inside the tissue favorable for multiplying and that results in infection. SSIs present with symptoms of local swelling, pus formation, and fever.

Respiratory Infections

Respiratory infections are also common hospital-acquired infections. Patients who receive artificial ventilation and have an endotracheal or tracheostomy tube in situ or get medication through inhalation (nebulization) commonly acquire these infections. In ICUs, a large proportion of critically ill patients are on mechanical ventilation. Through contaminated masks or oxygen tubing, they can get infections. Many patients admitted to the ICU are immuno-compromised and that further increases their chances of catching these infections. A patient with a respiratory infection may present with symptoms of a cough and fever.

Blood Infections

Blood infections are caused by contaminated invasive devices like injection needles, infusion cannula, and CVP catheters. Although administration of injections and intravenous infusion are simple and common procedures, they can transmit infecting organisms to vital organs through the circulatory system. When patients are on intravenous fluids therapy for a long period, healthcare providers tend to become careless about required aseptic precautions and no-touch techniques. A patient with a blood infection may present with the history of fever.

Preventing Hospital-Acquired Infections

To prevent infections in a hospital, actions are required on three fronts:

- Clinical procedures and practices
- Hospital environment
- Isolation of certain patients

Clinical Procedures and Practices

Clinical procedures like catheterization, surgeries, artificial ventilation, and intravenous infusion pose a risk of infection to patients. Infection can be caused if the medical devices used in these procedures are not sterile or if service providers do not follow proper aseptic techniques.

Medical Devices Used in Clinical Procedures

In 1968, Dr. Earle Spaulding classified the items used in patient care into the following three categories:

- Critical items
- Semicritical items
- Noncritical items

Critical Items

Critical items are those that invade a patient's tissue or blood vessels. Syringe needles, infusion cannulas, surgical instruments, cardiac catheters, and implants are critical items. They should be totally free of all microorganisms when used on patients. Sterilization is the process whereby such inanimate objects are rendered free of all microorganisms. Sterilization can be achieved through the following methods:

■ Steam sterilization
■ Gas sterilization
■ Chemical sterilization

Steam sterilization: Steam under pressure or autoclaving is the most cost-effective and most commonly used method of sterilization of surgical instruments and linen. It is performed in a machine known as an "autoclave." An autoclave has a metallic chamber. Instruments that are to be sterilized are wrapped in paper or cloth and placed in a drum. Gauze pieces, drapes, or cut sheets are placed directly in the drums. The drums with their holes open are placed in the chamber of the autoclave. The lid of the chamber is closed airtight. The chamber is filled with steam at a temperature of 121°C at 15 pounds of pressure. After 20–30 minutes of exposure to the steam, the items become sterilized and are taken out. Twenty minutes of exposure is the minimum requirement for the items that are placed directly in the drums. However, packed instruments need a longer exposure time of 30 minutes. After the required exposure to steam, the heating system is switched off, the autoclave's lid is opened, and drums are taken out. Steam is allowed to escape from the drums so that the items, particularly the linen does not become damp. Thereafter, the holes of the drums are closed. Then the sterile items are ready to use. They are handled using a no-touch technique.

Gas sterilization: Thermo-sensitive medical devices such as cardiac catheters are damaged by heat; therefore, they cannot be sterilized by autoclaving. They are sterilized with ethylene oxide (ETO) gas, which is a toxic and expensive gas. Therefore, it is suitable to sterilize only expensive items such as cardiac catheters. It is not cost-effective to sterilize inexpensive items like ventilation masks or oxygen tubing. Presterilized disposable items are a better option. An ETO sterilizer machine has an airtight chamber and the packed items to be sterilized are placed in it, and an ETO cartridge is fitted into the machine. One cartridge is required for each cycle. The chamber gets filled with ETO gas, which kills microorganisms, if any, associated with the medical devices. However, in this process, some gas particles also become attached to the medical devices. Since ETO is a highly toxic gas, the medical devices must be made totally free of gas particles before they are used on patients. This is done by subjecting the sterilized medical devices to forced ventilation. Ventilation blows away the ETO particles from the surface of the sterilized medical devices. This process takes several hours. One cycle of ETO sterilization is pretty long, about 8–12 hours. The high cost and long duration of the cycle are the major disadvantages of ETO.

Chemical sterilization: Chemical sterilization can be achieved by immersing the medical devices in 2% glutaraldehyde for 6–8 hours.

Semicritical Items

Semicritical items are those which do not invade a patient's tissue, but come in contact with the mucous membrane. Ventilation masks, urinary catheters, and endoscopes are the examples of semicritical items. As the mucous membrane is resistant to bacterial spores, it is not necessary to kill the spores associated with semicritical items, and that saves on costs significantly.

The process of making inanimate objects devoid of all microorganisms except spores is known as disinfection. Disinfection can be achieved through the following methods:

- Boiling
- Chemical disinfection

Boiling: Semicritical items like syringes, ventilation masks, urinary catheters, and oxygen tubing can be disinfected by boiling them at 100°C for 20 minutes. This is called high-level disinfection (HLD). This is an inexpensive method but presterilized disposable products are even more cost-effective, and therefore popular.

Chemical method: When medical devices are immersed in 2% glutaraldehyde for 20 minutes, all organisms except bacterial spores are killed resulting in high-level disinfection (HLD). Glutaraldehyde is an expensive chemical and is commonly used to disinfect scopes, such as endoscopes, arthroscopes, and laparoscopes, which have optical systems that are heat sensitive. It should be noted that endoscopes are semicritical items as they enter the intestine and come in contact with mucosa without invading tissues; but arthroscopes and laparoscopes are critical instruments since they invade a patient's tissue. Laparoscopes commonly used in tubal-ligation procedures are treated through HLD with 2% glutaraldehyde, at least in developing countries. Surprisingly, there are no indications of transmission of significant infections through this practice. Presently, this is an accepted practice.

If the glutaraldehyde exposure is increased to 6–10 hours, even spores are killed resulting in sterilization of the devices.

Noncritical Items

Noncritical items don't invade a patient's tissue or come in contact with their mucosa. They can, however, come in contact with a patient's intact skin. Bed sheets, patient furniture, stethoscopes, ECG electrodes, and the walls and floor of a room are examples of noncritical items. Noncritical items may harbor microorganisms, but these organisms generally do not cause any harm to the person exposed to them because of one's protective skin. Noncritical items need to be kept clean. Washing them with detergent and water is generally sufficient to prevent infections. The tiles on the walls of ICUs or operating rooms also require washing with detergent and water, and no chemical is required. Phenyl used for wet mopping of the floors is not likely to kill microorganisms as it is highly diluted. In fact, there is no need to kill microorganisms on the floor of a room. Phenyl is more of a deodorant.

Table 15.1   Risk of Infection from Commonly Encountered Items

High Risk of Infection	Moderate Risk of Infection	Low Risk of Infection	No Risk of Infection
Humidifier	Air filters	Suction apparatus	Toilets
Nebulizer	Inhaled medication	Sink	Flowers
Endoscopes	Ventilators	Shower	Carpets
Contaminated germicides	Bronchoscope	Pigeon droppings	ECG electrode
Food	Dialysis water		
Construction work	Bed mattress		
	Potable water		
	Tub immersion		

Protocols for treating patient care items through sterilization, high-level disinfection, or washing are generally based on Spaulding's classification. However, a study found a high chance of infection from some of the semicritical and even noncritical items as shown in Table 15.1.

Thus, depending on the risk of infection associated with an item, appropriate method of treatment should be used.

Clinical Practices

While carrying out clinical procedures, service providers must follow standard practices, such as hand washing and "no-touch techniques."

Hand washing: Before the mid-nineteenth century, people were not aware of the existence of microorganisms. They had no idea that certain diseases can be caused by microorganisms present in the environment. Thus, there was no concept of infection and infectious disease. Semmelweis, a practicing obstetrician, noticed that women who had prolonged labor had a higher incidence of puerperal fever. He suspected that the fever could have been caused by vaginal examinations. In the case of a prolonged labor, more numbers of vaginal examinations might be required to assess the progress of labor. Semmelweis asked his student doctors to wash their hands with lime before and after examining a patient. This practice led to a significant reduction in the incidence of puerperal fever and that proved his hypothesis. It is interesting to note that medical professionals accepted the findings of Semmelweis only after about 100 years.

Hand washing by service providers is known to be the single most important practice to prevent hospital-acquired infections. A normal hand wash with soap or detergent can wash away most organisms lying on the surface of the skin. However, 15%–20% of organisms can remain inside hair follicles and some of them can migrate to the surface of the skin during sweating. During hand washing, soap should be applied liberally and scrubbed thoroughly, particularly in nail beds. This process should be continued for at least 30 seconds. The Center for Disease Control and Prevention (CDC), Atlanta, an authority on infection prevention in healthcare settings, recommends hand washing under the following circumstances:

- Before wearing sterile gloves and after removing them
- Before and after all invasive procedures
- Before and after touching wounds or invasive devices
- Before and after caring of susceptible or infected patients
- Between contact with patients in high-risk areas like ICUs

Before surgical procedures, service providers are required to scrub their hands and forearms for a minimum 3 minutes. An alcohol rub is also very effective in the hand sanitization of service providers. A hand scrub followed by an alcohol rub is a standard practice in operating rooms.

Standard Precautions

Standard precautions or universal precautions are primarily aimed at the safety of service providers, although they are also useful for patients. They have been formulated based on the concept that human blood and body fluids can be potentially infectious, and whenever there is a risk of becoming exposed to them, service providers should use appropriate barriers to protect themselves. Body fluids include semen, vaginal secretions, pericardial, pleural, peritoneal, synovial, and cerebrospinal fluid, urine, feces, sputum, tears, sweat or vomit. Barriers that can be used by service providers to protect themselves from exposure to blood or the body fluids of a client are

- Gloves
- Masks
- Gown
- Goggles
- Head gear

Standard precautions, in addition to barriers, advocate hand washing and precautions against sharp injuries. Service providers with exudative lesions should refrain from providing direct patient care. Barriers used in clinical practice are explained subsequently.

Gloves: Latex gloves are the most cost-effective and commonly used gloves. They are considered suitable for use in operating rooms and other patient care areas. A study found seepage of blood in 20% of surgeons' gloves when a surgery was of more than 2 hours. After 6 hours of use, seepage was found in 80% of gloves. The CDC recommends the use of single-latex gloves for procedures of less than 2 hours duration, and double gloving for procedures lasting for more than 2 hours. Double gloving is also useful if blood loss is expected to be more than 100 ml. A study reported that most of the surgeons found double gloving comfortable and they did not feel any impairment in their tactile sensations. There is a standard technique of wearing sterile gloves without touching its external surface, which should be followed diligently by the service providers. Gloves treated with chlorine or acrylates provide a slick surface that does not require powdering, but these gloves are expensive.

Mask: A normal person expels particles while breathing or speaking. The expulsion of particles is higher while coughing, and much higher while sneezing. Some of these particles contain bacteria. A mask can stop most of these particles. Reusable double-layer cotton fabric masks are as effective as synthetic masks. The mask should fully cover the mouth and nose of the person.

Gown: Surgical team members are required to wear sterile gowns so that their sterile gloved hands do not touch any unsterile garment. Secondly, from the bare skin of service providers, skin fragments disperse in the environment and some of these fragments carry organisms, which can transmit infections, particularly in operating rooms and ICUs. Cotton gowns reduce the dispersal of skin particles by 30%. Synthetic gowns are more effective but expensive. If a surgery lasts less than 2 hours and the bleeding is less than 100 ml, the CDC recommends that surgical team members wear single-layer cotton gowns. However, if the procedure is of a longer duration, blood loss is expected to be more, or the procedure involves the chest or abdominal cavity, a plastic coating on the arms and chest of the gown is recommended. Service providers are required to follow the proper technique of wearing a sterile gown without touching its external sterile surface.

Shoe covers: Street shoes can be highly contaminated with dust and fecal matter and, therefore, are not allowed inside the operating rooms and ICUs. One is required to change into clean slippers before entering these facilities. These slippers should be washed with detergent and water every day. Paper shoe covers are also effective but expensive. Secondly, they produce dust by friction, which can clog air filters in specialized operating rooms.

Head gear: A few outbreaks of surgical site infections were reportedly caused by personnel who were carriers of the *Staphylococcus aureus* bacteria on their scalp. The effectiveness of caps in preventing such infections is not well established. Still, surgical team members are advised to wear caps inside the operating theater to prevent their hair from falling on to the surgical site.

Eye protection: Unprotected eyes are extremely vulnerable to splashes of blood from a surgical site. Protective eyewear is recommended in large surgeries or while conducting deliveries. Vision corrective glasses are not effective in protecting the eyes of a surgeon from such splashes.

Hospital Environment

The hospital environment plays an important role in preventing infections. This includes air, water, food, bed sheets, surfaces of furniture and equipment, and walls and floor of the rooms. The following measures can help maintaining a clean environment in a hospital:

Ventilation: Operating rooms and ICUs require special ventilation standards. Minor operating rooms, patient rooms, and other patient care areas should have either cross-ventilation or air conditioning.

Water: Water should be treated and made potable before distributing for drinking or cooking purpose. It should be tested periodically for the presence of coliform bacteria, hardness, and other contaminants, and corrective actions should be taken in case of abnormalities.

Kitchen cleanliness and food hygiene: Food is a significant source of infections in hospitals. The health of the food handlers is important. They should be closely monitored for their personal hygiene, nail beds, oozing wounds, and habits. They should take a daily bath and wear clean clothes and an apron. Their nails should be clipped. They should wash their hands religiously and wear clean gloves every time before handling food. There should be adequate hand washing facilities in the kitchen. Raw fruits and vegetables should be washed thoroughly before cooking. Cooking utensils, dishes, and the surfaces on which cutting and food processing is done should be clean. Adequate ventilation should be maintained in the kitchen area. Fly-proofing and insect-proofing of the kitchen may be required. Food trolleys should be cleaned every time before and after distributing food. Periodic checks for insects and rodents should be undertaken in food trolleys, kitchen appliances, and the kitchen area.

Housekeeping: Housekeeping generally refers to the cleaning and mopping of the floor, dusting, changing of bed linen, and disposing of waste. Good housekeeping is critical to prevent infections in hospitals. Dry mopping should not be done in hospitals as it causes the dispersal of dust particles that may contain microorganisms. Some of these organisms, such as tuberculosis bacteria and varicella are highly infectious and can transmit infections to patients, staff, and visitors. Frequent wet mopping of the floors should be done. If possible, hot water may be used for wet mopping. The floor and wall tiles of operating rooms and ICUs should be washed with detergent and water at least once a week. In a study, it was found that the quantum of microorganisms on the operating lights was as high as on the floor of the operating room. It is recommended that the operating room lights, operating table, instrument trolley, surface of patient furniture, window, and door panes should be wiped with a moist clean cloth every day.

Laundry precautions: Bed sheets on patient beds should be changed every day or whenever soiled. Normal linen can be washed with detergent and water, preferably hot water. The linen used by HIV-positive patients can also be reused after treatment and washing. It can be decontaminated by soaking it in 0.5% sodium hypochlorite solution for 10 minutes, followed by washing in hot water. Thereafter, it can be reused like any other linen.

Isolation of Infectious Patients

Highly infectious patients, like those suffering from tuberculosis or chickenpox patients, should be isolated to protect hospital staff and other patients from them. On the other hand, immuno-compromised patients like those suffering from leukemia, patients on anticancer drugs, or critically ill patients should be isolated to protect them from other patients and staff.

Infection Prevention Program in a Hospital

A typical infection prevention program in a hospital or healthcare facility comprises the following components:

- Developing clinical protocols and standard operating procedures (SOPs)
- Implementing the defined protocols and SOPs
- Establishing a system for surveillance
- Staff training

Developing Protocols and SOPs

Hospital infection prevention committee: Every hospital should have an infection prevention committee headed preferably by the head of clinical services. A senior microbiologist, infection-prevention nurse, and interested clinicians can be the members. The committee is responsible for formulating clinical protocols and SOPs to prevent infections in various patient care areas. A few examples of SOPs are given here:

General

Hand washing: Before and after attending to any patient, service providers will wash their hands.

Antibiotic policy: Out of every 100 samples of blood and body fluids received in the hospital laboratory, one sample will be subjected to a culture and sensitivity test. Based on the findings, the antibiotic policy of the hospital will be developed. Information on the efficacy of common antibiotics will be shared with the consultants, and they will be encouraged to prescribe only the efficacious antibiotics. The policy will be revised annually.

Safe water and food hygiene: Water will be treated and made potable before distributing for drinking or cooking purposes. Food handlers will be medically examined every month. Samples of water and food will be sent for testing quarterly and corrective actions will be taken in case of an abnormal report.

Disposal of waste: Infectious waste, general waste, sharp objects, and plastics will be segregated at the point of generation. Infectious waste will be sent for incineration; sharp objects will be collected in puncture-proof container and sent to be deep buried; plastics will be decontaminated, mutilated, and sent for recycling; and general waste will be sent for municipal disposal. More details are given in Chapter 16, "Biomedical Waste Management."

Housekeeping services: As discussed earlier in this chapter.

Vaccination of personnel: All service providers involved in direct patient care will be immunized against hepatitis B.

Operating Rooms

Shaving before surgery: Hair on the surgical site will not be shaved on the previous day or night. It will be clipped. If very necessary, it may be shaved immediately before the surgery.

Prophylactic antibiotic administration: A bolus dose of broad-spectrum antibiotic will be given intravenously half an hour before the incision of the surgery to prevent postoperative infections.

Postoperative antibiotics: Postoperative antibiotics will not be advised routinely.

Trolley exchange system: Operating room and ward trolleys will be exchanged while shifting the patients in and out of operating rooms.

Fumigation: Fumigation will not be done routinely in the operating rooms. However, in case of an epidemic of postoperative infections, the operating rooms may be fumigated.

Intensive Care Units

Hand washing: Before and after attending to patients, service providers will sanitize their hands with alcohol. Alcohol rub will be made available at each bedside.

Protocol for visitors: Visitors to patients in ICUs will change to ICU slippers before entering the patient care area. The ICU slippers will be washed every day with detergent and water.

Urinary catheters: Patients' urinary catheters will be changed every fortnight.

Central Sterile Supply Department

Quality of sterilization: Each pack loaded in autoclaves will have a chemical indicator—bowie dick's tape. Every quarter, biological tests will be carried out for each autoclave and ETO machine.

Other Patient Care Areas

Cheatle's forceps: The Cheatle's forceps and stand will be autoclaved every day before putting them into use. Cheatle's forceps will not be kept immersed in savlon solution.

Blood Bank

Screening of blood: Each collected blood unit will be tested for HIV, HBV, HCV, syphilis, and malaria, and the contaminated units will be discarded.

Implementation

A practical approach to implementing an infection prevention program in a hospital is to begin in a few selected areas and gradually expand. As discussed earlier, unconscious patients admitted to ICUs; patients who have undergone surgery, and catheterized patients are at a higher risk of acquiring hospital infections. Accordingly, the facilities where such patients are treated can be the priority areas of infection prevention program:

- Operating rooms
- ICUs
- Delivery rooms
- Post operative wards

An infection prevention committee should develop clinical protocols and SOPs for each area. Important SOPs should be displayed at strategic points. Service providers including doctors, nurses, housekeeping staff, hospital aides, pantry staff, and security staff working in these areas should be trained on issues relevant to their work. Required logistics support should be provided; for example, adequate hand washing facilities should be made available. Similarly, if visitors are required to change their slippers before entering the ICU, the slippers should be available at a designated place at the entrance of the ICU.

Surveillance System

An infection prevention nurse should be appointed for every 250 beds in a hospital. She should be dedicated full-time to infection prevention activities and should not have any patient care responsibilities. The infection prevention nurse is required to perform the following functions:

- Monitor culture reports
- Make clinical rounds and collect data

- Analyze data
- Investigate important cases
- Take corrective actions

Monitor culture reports: The infection prevention nurse scrutinizes the culture reports of all samples of blood and other body fluids that are tested in the microbiology laboratory and pulls out all positive reports.

Make clinical rounds and collect data: The infection prevention nurse makes clinical rounds in selected wards and tracks the patients whose culture reports were positive. She meets them, checks their past clinical records and interacts with the ward nurse or treating doctor to determine if they were free of the said infection earlier and had developed a new infection.

In addition, she can screen postoperative patients to identify if someone developed pus or swelling on his surgical site or if someone developed a fever. She can take the history of patients on ventilators to find out those who developed a new cough, sputum, or fever. Diagnosis of hospital-acquired infections can be made on the following criteria: (Table 15.2).

The infection prevention nurse also records whether the patients with positive culture reports are on antibiotic treatment or not.

Analyze the data: The nurse determines the total number of patients of each category (or denominator) to calculate the rate of hospital-acquired infections in each critical patient care areas.

Investigate: In areas that have a high hospital-acquired infection rate, the infection prevention nurse should conduct an investigation to identify the source of infection, responsible organism, and its mode of transmission. She can collect samples from the relevant suspected critical or semicritical items like surgical instruments, ventilation masks, dialysis

Table 15.2 Criteria for Identifying New Infections in Patients

Site of Infection	Criteria	Source of Information
Urine	Bacterial count 10^5 colonies/ml, fever	Laboratory
Postoperative wounds	Pus at the incision site, fever	Clinical picture
Respiratory system	History of cough, new sputum production, fever	Clinical picture
Blood	Positive blood culture report, fever	Laboratory
Gastrointestinal system	Unexplained diarrhea for >2 days	Clinical picture
Liver	Yellow urine, deranged liver function tests	Clinical picture, laboratory

water, air conditioning ducts, or mattresses. It should be understood that there is no point in taking routine samples from the air of operating rooms or tiles on the walls of ICUs as they are likely to be contaminated. They have to be cleaned or washed regularly whether organisms are found in them or not.

Take corrective actions: Based on the findings of the investigation, corrective actions are taken. The infection prevention nurse should share the findings of her investigation with the heads of department, and orient the staff concerned on the relevant issues to prevent infections.

Bibliography

C. Glen Mayhall, *Hospital Epidemiology and Infection Control*, Lippincott Williams, Philadelphia, PA, 1996.

Chapter 16

Biomedical Waste Management

Anything that we do not intend to use is waste. Large multi-speciality hospitals produce about 2–3 kg of waste per bed per day. Smaller hospitals and nursing homes produce less, depending upon the number of surgeries and clinical tests and the quantity of disposables used by them.

Hazards of Hospital Waste

The infectious waste generated in hospitals can transmit infections or diseases to users or service providers, handlers of waste, and the community. It can also pollute the environment. Sharp wastes are mainly responsible for transmitting infections. Nurses and surgeons occasionally get needle-prick injuries. A study found that two-thirds of nurses in a hospital had sustained needle-prick injuries at some stage during their career. Recapping of syringes should be discouraged as the majority of needle prick injuries occur during this process. Waste handlers often get injured by sharp objects such as needles and blades. Sharp-object injuries can transmit the human immunodeficiency virus (HIV), hepatitis B (HBV), or hepatitis C (HBC). Microbiological wastes like culture plates, slides, and leftover samples of body fluids are potentially hazardous, although not many cases of infection have been reported through them.

Types of Hospital Waste

Hospitals produce both infectious and noninfectious waste.

Infectious Waste

- Infectious solid waste: Cotton swabs, gauze, and dressings soiled with blood or body fluids
- Sharp objects: Syringe needles, infusion set needles, scalpel blades, broken glassware
- Human anatomical/pathological waste: Tissues removed during surgeries, amputated body parts, placenta, tissues collected for biopsy or histopathological examination
- Microbiological waste: Culture material, leftover samples of blood, urine, stool, and pus

Noninfectious Waste

Noninfectious waste includes kitchen waste, packing materials, and paper.

Need for Segregation of Waste

Out of the total waste generated in a hospital, only 10% is infectious. It is only the infectious waste that has to be treated in a special way, which is expensive; noninfectious waste can be managed like any other domestic or municipal waste. Most hospitals fail to segregate infectious waste from the noninfectious. As a result, all waste has to be treated as infectious, and that raises the cost of waste treatment ten-fold. The second important consideration is that plastic constitutes about 10%–15% of total hospital waste. Plastic waste cannot be burned or incinerated as it produces toxic or carcinogenic gases. Thus, segregation of different types of waste is of paramount importance. This has to be done at the point of generation of waste. In other words, the person who uses an item and generates the waste should discard it in an appropriate container.

Segregation of Waste

Hospital waste can be segregated based on the following four categories:

1. Infectious waste: Yellow container
2. Sharp waste: Puncture-proof container
3. Plastic waste: Red container
4. General waste: Black container

Infectious waste: Soiled cotton, gauze, bandages, and anatomical waste are examples of infectious waste. Infectious and microbiological waste can be collected in yellow bags. They can be treated by incineration. Since plastic bags are chlorinated, they produce toxic gases on burning. Nonchlorinated yellow bags are also available, they are expensive, but they do not produce toxic gases on incineration.

Sharp objects: As discussed earlier, sharp objects such as needles, blades, and broken glass are potentially dangerous to handlers; therefore, no effort should be made to decontaminate or mutilate them. Sharp objects can be collected in a puncture-proof container. The container, when filled, can be sent for deep burial or incineration.

Plastic waste: Plastic items like infusion sets, syringes, tubing, and wrappers cannot be burned or incinerated as they produce carcinogenic gases like dioxin and furan on burning. Plastic should be decontaminated by soaking it in a 1% sodium hypochlorite solution. After decontamination, it may be mutilated or cut into pieces to prevent reuse. The decontaminated and mutilated plastics can be recycled.

General waste: Items like packing materials and kitchen waste can be collected in black bags that can be sent along with municipal waste for sanitary landfill.

Technologies for Treatment of Waste

Infectious wastes can be treated through one of the subsequent methods.

Incineration

An incinerator is a kind of furnace that has two chambers lined with heat-resistant bricks. One or more burners are installed in each chamber to produce a high temperature. The waste is loaded in the primary chamber where the temperature is raised to 850°C and the waste is burned into ashes and gases. The gases are then released into the secondary chamber where they are further heated to a temperature of 1050°C. Such a high temperature renders them harmless. The gases are then passed through water and liberated into the environment at a height of 30 feet above the ground through a chimney. If the temperature in the chambers remains below the prescribed standards, the gases liberated may be toxic. Overloading of the primary chamber is a common reason for its inability to achieve the desired temperature. Incinerators can run on electricity or diesel. Some incinerators, after initial ignition with electricity, run on diesel.

An important advantage of incinerators is that human body parts are burned into ashes, which reduces social or ethical considerations. Furthermore, the total volume of the waste is significantly reduced. The ash produced in the plant is safe and relatively convenient to dispose of. The disadvantages include the high cost of equipment and the high cost of running the incinerator. The incinerator emits smoke and gases that are often a matter of concern for the people living in the surrounding areas. Plastics and the items disinfected by a hypochlorite solution cannot be treated in the incinerator as they produce toxic gases.

Contracting out to waste management agencies: Professional waste management agencies collect waste from hospitals, transport it, and treat it by incineration. They have incinerators installed in the outskirts of cities. Even if waste management is contracted out to an external agency, the management of the hospital is accountable for the transport, treatment, and disposal of the waste as per guidelines.

Sanitary landfilling: Sanitary landfilling and deep burial are accepted methods for disposal of waste, where land is available for this purpose. Sanitary landfilling is done by dumping the waste in a low-lying area far away from habitation. The area should be protected by a fence to prevent access to rag pickers and animals. After each day's filling, the waste should be covered with a layer of soil to prevent access to flies, rodents, and insects. The pressure of the overlying earth and waste produces heat in the deeper layers, which converts the waste into innocuous material.

Microwaves: A microwave used for treating waste is similar to one used in a kitchen, but it is of a very large size. The equipment is expensive and consumes much power. An important disadvantage of a microwave is that the appearance and volume of the waste treated by it remain unchanged. Thus, even though the body parts, blood stained cotton, and pus soaked gauze pieces are rendered noninfectious by a microwave, their appearance and volume remain the same.

Ethical considerations and their further disposal remains a challenge.

Autoclaves: Autoclaves are commonly used for treating microbiological waste in laboratories. Autoclaves also have the disadvantages of microwaves. Autoclaves are discussed in Chapter 15 "Infection Prevention."

Role of Pollution Control Boards

In some countries, Central and State Pollution Control Boards (CPCB) are responsible for regulating the management of hospital waste, which includes collection, transport, handling, and treatment. Board officials visit a hospital periodically to inspect the system for segregation of waste in various patient care areas and the safety measures observed by the waste handlers. CPCB's approval is needed for installing an incinerator in the hospital campus. Board officials check whether the equipment meets specifications and has been installed properly. They can check the temperature in each chamber of the incinerator and collect samples of the gases from its chimney.

Chapter 17

Marketing Management

Earlier, hospitals were mostly owned by governments or charitable organizations, and their services were either free or subsidized. People, who were in need and had access to these institutions, utilized their services. Since most of these hospitals were already overcrowded there was no need for them to attract more clients. Traditionally, these hospitals used to employ a public relations officer to manage public grievances. This was important, particularly to cover up unfavorable incidents occurring in the hospital. Also, they played a key role in publicizing any special surgery performed in the hospital or any feat achieved by the hospital. They maintained a relationship with the press to get such news published, and were also required to liaise with the government to get possible benefits.

When corporate or for-profit hospitals came up, they charged a fee for their services, which could not be afforded by everybody. Hospitals survive and thrive only if people utilize their services. So, the need arose for the marketing of hospital services.

There have been discussions on the ethics of marketing healthcare services. Some consider it unethical on the part of hospitals or medical practitioners to advertise their services. Gradually, an understanding is developing that there is nothing wrong in making the public aware of the services available in a hospital. Similarly, it is worth informing people when a leading medical professional joins a hospital or new high-tech equipment is installed. In other words, providing factual information to people about healthcare services without any exaggeration is not considered unethical.

4Ps of Marketing

Traditionally marketing is considered to be a product of 4Ps:

1. Product
2. Price
3. Place
4. Promotion

Product: The quality of a product or service is an important consideration for the clients to purchase it. The quality should be of a pre-decided level and provide the client with a good value for money.

Price: The price of services should be affordable to the public. The price is determined by both internal and external factors. Internal factors include the cost incurred by the organization in providing the services. External market forces include the dynamics of demand and supply. The price offered by a competitor acts as an influence.

Place: Deciding where the services should be offered is a critical decision. Offering services, even of a high quality at a location where people are not able to afford it can prove to be futile.

Promotion: The process of communicating the value of a service or product to people is known as "promotion." Advertising is one of the ways of promoting. The difference between marketing and advertising should be understood. Marketing is a broader concept and advertising is a component of marketing.

Advertising involves developing persuasive messages and sending it across to the intended audience through selected media.

Modern Concept of Marketing

Promoters used to establish businesses based on their financial and technical capacity and possible financial returns. For example, people with an engineering background established manufacturing factories, people with expertise in catering started catering businesses or set up restaurants, doctors established clinics. Over time some flourishing clinics expanded into hospitals. After setting up a business, if the promoters felt that the uptake of services was not adequate, they invested money on "marketing" to increase their clientele. Nowadays business organizations adopt a different marketing approach as explained subsequently:

Identifying the Needs of People

Modern marketing focuses on people and their needs. The "needs of the people" are the starting point of any business. To understand the relationship between the needs of people and the business, let us take a few examples.

The telecom industry in India was once entirely state-owned, international and inter-province telephone dialing facilities were available solely in government telephone exchanges. Opening the sector to private players expanded the existing network and increased connectivity in the country. Private telephone service providers flourished. As technology developed, mobile phones became cheaper. Marked by their convenience and cheap call rates, they came to be widely used. As a result, the businesses of private telephone booth operators slowed, and eventually shut down.

On another front, 50 years ago, there weren't many restaurants in India as the masses simply didn't have enough money for this. As the economic conditions of people improved, they began eating out in restaurants. As a result, restaurants mushroomed all over the country and did good business. Improved economic conditions were supplemented by a changed lifestyle that led to obesity. A new need emerged: the need to remain fit. Accordingly, fitness centers and private gyms have sprung up and are profitable. The situation is similar for beauty salons. It becomes evident that people's needs drive business. Accordingly, some marketing experts added a 5th "P" to the 4Ps of marketing, denoting "People." Businesses that are planned and designed to fulfill the needs of people are more likely to succeed, and those are the fundamentals of modern marketing.

In addition, healthcare services should be

1. Accessible to the people for whom they are intended
2. Available to them
3. Acceptable
4. Affordable

These are known as the 4A's of marketing.

Creating a Need-Based Service

Let us see how healthcare services evolved according to the needs of people. People earlier depended on family physicians. They took pride in being associated with a popular family physician. Gradually, as their needs evolved, they wanted to know more about their medical problems and receive accurate treatment. They began to consult specialists, have the required diagnostic tests done, and obtain evidence-based treatment. This increased the demand for specialist doctors and hospitals.

It was assumed that cardiovascular diseases or heart attacks, strokes, and cancer were diseases of affluent countries. It has since been realized that the incidence of these diseases is increasing at an alarming rate in India. This has led to cardiac and neurology centers to spring up, particularly in cities. These centers have greater profitability compared with general hospitals.

Now a days, cancer hospitals are doing good business due to the increased prevalence of the disease, a higher client load, and the increased paying capacity of people. This development came after a time when cancer treatment was not considered a lucrative business, since the investment required was high and returns were poor. Similarly, as the prevalence of diabetes is shooting up, the number of diabetes clinics and laboratories is growing.

General wards in hospitals accommodated 20–30 patients in a dormitory. Patients did not mind sharing a room or a common toilet. This has been replaced by an increasing need for privacy; people need an individual room with an attached toilet in a hospital and they are willing to pay. So, new hospitals have been designed to have mostly single-occupancy private rooms. The time when the average duration of a patient's stay in the hospital was 7 days or more gave way to a time when this duration has reduced to 3 days in many hospitals. People want shorter stays in the hospital. Of course, improved technology favors fast turnover. Day care surgeries and day care procedures are gaining popularity. People do not like large scars from surgery; therefore, keyhole surgeries are becoming popular. Lately, cosmetic surgeries, vision correction surgeries, and weight reduction surgeries are picking up as per changes in perceptions of beauty.

The proportion of the geriatric population is increasing in many countries, and elderly people have a higher prevalence of degenerative disorders. Accordingly, chronic care centers or geriatric nursing homes are springing up. When elderly people fall sick, their children or family members may not have the time to look after them. They want to have them admitted in a well-equipped hospital where their needs can be taken care of. Accordingly, the proportion of ICU beds is increasing in corporate hospitals. Their demand as well as their occupancy is high and hospitals make greater profits on ICU beds as compared with other indoor beds.

Increasing Visibility of the Organization and Services

Once services have been set up to fulfill the needs of people, the next step is to generate awareness about the services. Providing information to potential clients is the key to creating demand for services. Potential clients should get information about types of services available, their quality, and value. And some of them may consider utilizing them. The concept of "early adopters" says that in every community there are some people who are willing to experiment with new things or purchase new services.

Who should receive information about the services? Who are the potential clients of a hospital? Very few organizations can think of providing services to the entire population. Tea, coffee, and soft drinks are popular in many countries, and the vast majority of people consume these products on a regular basis. So, their manufacturers target an entire population. On the other hand, services like healthcare are targeted to specific populations in specific geographical areas. This is known as market segmentation.

Market segmentation: Every business caters to a specific segment of the population in terms of their geographical location, age, sex, and vocation, health-seeking behavior, paying capacity, insurance status, and so on. For example, infertility clinics target rich and young married couples. Joint replacement centers target elderly clients. Eye correction centers may target adolescents. Cosmetic surgery centers may cater to middle-aged women.

Economically poor communities have different needs: their fertility is often high, they need antenatal care, safe deliveries, and postnatal care services. Diarrhea, pneumonia, and vaccine preventable diseases are common in their children;

malaria, dengue fever, and other communicable diseases are common in adults. In addition, their paying capacity is low; so, their health-seeking behavior can be different. While planning healthcare services for them, these factors need to be taken into account.

Not only are the people who need and utilize the services of a healthcare organization important, the people who buy the services or who influence the decision of buying services are equally important. For example, when a child falls sick, her mother or family members decide the service provider or the hospital from where they will seek services. Corporate houses that care for the health of their employees can be potential clients for preventive health checkup services. A high-tech surgical facility can think of targeting international clients.

Promotion

Information about available hospitals or healthcare services can be provided to potential clients through many channels. Billboards can be displayed in prominent locations. Leaflets can be distributed through newspapers, pharmacies, laboratories, or through special messengers. Advertisements in television or radio have high credibility and provide wide coverage, but they are expensive.

Some of new hospitals arrange to provide transportation to bring patients from rural or remote areas and to drop them back.

Free medical checkup camps for elderly people or free checkups of blood pressure or blood sugar, and so on organized by hospitals, are a common method of promoting a hospital. It is expected that the people who avail of the free services, will become familiar with the hospital and other services that are available. Gradually, they will start availing of the paid services when required.

Referral Linkages

For a hospital, particularly a specialized hospital, an important category of clients is the practitioners who can refer their patients. These practitioners may be family physicians, practitioners of other systems of medicine, or unqualified practitioners. Peripheral health centers, pharmacies, or laboratories are also important sources of referral. There have been ethical considerations regarding payment of commissions to the referring practitioners. For example, if a practitioner refers a patient to a hospital, where the patient is operated on, should the hospital pay a commission, say 10–15% of the amount recovered from the patient to the referring practitioner? Well, this is considered unethical, even if the referral was for a genuine reason and the patient received appropriate treatment at the hospital. This is because such a practice can encourage practitioners to refer patients without a genuine need.

Referred patients receiving appropriate treatment at an appropriate price is a good enough reason for practitioners to refer their patients to a particular hospital. Besides, there are several ways hospitals can show appreciation for a practitioner's referral. The hospital can provide feedback to the practitioner about the ailment of the referred patient and their treatment plan. This is possible if the hospital captures the data of the referring practitioner at the time of the client's registration. Front office staff will have to be trained to do so. Secondly, visiting consultants in referral hospitals are generally very busy; they are not likely to take the trouble of contacting the referring practitioner and informing him about a client. The hospital may engage a full-time medical officer or an experienced nurse, who can provide feedback to the referring practitioners. They can be the first point of contact, or liaison officers, for the referring practitioners.

The hospital can organize continuing medical education (CME) programs for the practitioners of the area. The liaison officer may orient them to various facilities available in the hospital. Sessions can be organized on topics of common interest for the practitioners. Practitioners should have an opportunity to interact with hospital consultants over a cup of tea or refreshments. This will allow them to feel honored and take pride in being affiliated with the hospital.

Client Relationship Management

The key challenge in private hospitals is to retain the clients who visit them for the first time. Some marketing experts feel frustrated that they generate demand for services and get clients, but the organization fails to provide quality services. Clients become dissatisfied and do not return. Client relationship management is a big challenge, which unfortunately many organizations do not acknowledge and address.

The clients, on their arrival to a hospital expect someone to attend to them promptly, behave in a friendly manner, direct them through the next steps, explain how much time it will take to get the service, and tell them how much it would cost. During their interaction, medical professionals must show their concern for the client's problem. They should clearly explain what the problem is or appears to be, how it might be confirmed, plans to treat it, and what the prognosis is. In this way, a long-term relationship is established with the clients. These issues are explained in detail in Chapter 7, "Patient Satisfaction."

Value for money: The clients should get value for their money. They should not expect to get a better service at the given price. In fact, they should get more than what they had expected. Some orthopedic hospitals provide the services of a physiotherapist at the client's home after discharge. Some hospitals arrange to get periodic blood sugar estimates done for their diabetes patients. The unique selling proposition (USP) of a business that differentiates itself from its competitors plays an important role in its success.

Creating Interest

Marketing techniques are also utilized to influence people's interests or preferences for a service. It is believed that they can even change people's behavior. For example, in the past there was no need for soft drinks, tea, or coffee but manufacturers created demand for these products, and now they are a regular requirement for a large number of people globally. People who keep mobile phones can see the "time" on their mobile phone screens and do not require a watch to know the time, but high-end watch companies, through advertisements, can generate demand for their products. People take pride in buying and wearing these watches. Similarly, demand is being created for certain healthcare services, such as cosmetic surgeries.

Bibliography

Philip Kotler et al., *Strategic Marketing for Health Care Organizations: Building a Customer Driven Health System*, Indianapolis, IN, Jossey-Bass, 2008.

Chapter 18

Demand Generation

Marketing is aimed at increasing an organization's profit by expanding its utilization of services or products. "For-profit organizations" generally utilize modern marketing techniques and processes. However, there is another dimension of marketing known as "social marketing." Social marketing is the process of bringing about positive changes in people's behavior or practices. It encourages them to adopt healthier lifestyles, and this is achieved by utilizing modern marketing techniques. For example, diarrhea is a common cause of death among children in economically weaker societies. Oral rehydration solution is an effective therapy for diarrhea. But, people do not use it because of their ignorance, misconceptions, or poor access. Utilization of oral rehydration solutions can be increased through social marketing. Through behavior change communication, mothers or caregivers of children can be encouraged to use oral rehydration solutions in case of diarrhea in children. Since social marketing is aimed at benefiting the community, it may not necessarily provide monetary benefits to the executing organization.

In various public health programs, social marketing has been used for promoting immunization in children and increasing contraceptive use, such as condoms, oral contraceptive pills, IUCD, or implants. Despite the availability of services like IUCD, implants, tubal ligations, or vasectomies in healthcare facilities, their utilization is often poor due to a lack of awareness and myths and misconceptions among people. Efforts can be made to generate a demand for these services. Let us take the example of vasectomy services and understand how we can generate demand.

Demand Generation for Vasectomy Services

Men's participation in family planning is poor in many developing countries. In these places, women assume this responsibility by using one of the available methods, such as oral contraceptive pills, IUCD, implants, or tubal ligation. For men, there are two methods of family planning: condoms and vasectomies. Lately condoms have gained importance due to their role in preventing HIV/AIDS, but vasectomies have continued to be neglected.

Vasectomy is a safe, simple, and effective method of permanent contraception. The no-scalpel vasectomy (NSV) is an improved technique over the conventional vasectomy. The NSV procedure can be completed within 20 minutes in an outpatient setting and the client can walk home after an hour of resting post procedure. He can resume strenuous work after 2 days.

Increasing men's participation in family planning has been a challenge for public health. Informing them about NSV being a safe, simple, and effective method has not been successful. Efforts made in the past to get them to understand and assume their responsibilities have not shown the desired results either. What can be done? How can men be encouraged to undergo NSVs? Before trying to bring about a change in peoples' behavior, we need to understand the reasons for the existing situation.

Why Don't Men Accept NSV?

It is a well-known fact that men, generally, do not accept NSVs as a method for family planning due to misconceptions about them causing weakness. They believe that after getting an NSV they will be unable to perform the rigorous manual labor that is necessary for them to earn their livelihood. Why do people relate NSVs to physical weakness? In-depth discussions with men and women revealed that although they speak of physical weakness, their main concern is in fact about sexual weakness. It is believed that during the procedure, since the tube carrying spermatic fluids is cut, there will be no ejaculation and sexual intercourse will no longer be pleasurable. It was also found that women were equally and sometimes more concerned. They feared the NSV affecting the erection and ejaculation of their husband, who would lose interest in sex. Instead they preferred to undergo tubal ligation over allowing their husbands to get an NSV. Even if some men showed interest in getting an NSV they were discouraged by their spouse.

Not only are community members shy about seeking clarification on issues related to erection and ejaculation, the outreach workers and healthcare service providers are equally hesitant to talk on the subject. In fact, some healthcare workers are not themselves very clear about it.

How Can NSV Acceptance Be Increased?

The only way to dispel misconceptions among people is to provide them with the correct information and if possible, with evidence. In case of NSVs, potential clients need to be explicitly informed that the NSV will not affect their erection and ejaculation. They will be able to enjoy sex as before. Their spouses need to be assured of the same as well. When this is clarified many men will come forward to accept NSV. This was a hypothesis that required testing.

Hypothesis Testing

It was decided to test this hypothesis in a project mode on a selected geographical area.

Interventions were designed, messages were developed in local language and pretested, and information materials were printed. A batch of outreach workers were oriented toward the facts about NSV. With the support of a simplified schematic diagram of the male anatomy, the process of ejaculation was explained. It was clarified that the sperm is produced in the testicles and the seminal fluid is produced in other glands (seminal vesicle and prostate). The ducts carrying sperm from the testicles are different from the ducts transporting seminal fluid. Sperm mix with the seminal fluid during ejaculation. In the NSV procedure only ducts carrying sperm are blocked. The other ducts that carry seminal fluid are not tampered with. Therefore, after undergoing an NSV, the ejaculation of the seminal fluid will occur normally and the NSV recipient will continue to experience the same pleasure. The only difference will be that their seminal fluid will be devoid of sperm that can cause conception and pregnancy. It was also clarified that there will be no effect on the erection or hardness of the male organ because of NSV.

The need to discuss these issues explicitly with potential couples was emphasized to the outreach workers. They were provided with job aids having a schematic diagram of the male anatomy to initiate the discussion. Using roleplay, efforts were made to make them confident and comfortable in discussing this sensitive issue with an intended audience. Male workers were asked to discuss this with potential clients, and female workers were asked to discuss this with their spouses.

Some healthcare service providers or public health experts were apprehensive that in conservative societies it may not be appropriate to talk about sex-related issues like erection, ejaculation, or pleasure. They feared a reaction from social activists or the media. However, on pretesting it was realized that their worry was unfounded.

Due respect was given to the concept of informed and voluntary decision-making while communicating with potential clients. The outreach workers were told to provide information on all available methods of contraception to eligible couples. Only those who showed interest in NSV were provided with a detailed account. No efforts were made to show NSV being better than other methods.

During pretesting, when the outreach workers were interacting with potential clients, their supervisors closely observed the process. It was found that despite training; only 10–15% outreach workers were able to discuss these issues frankly with the intended audience. The rest of the 80–85% workers only conveyed a broad message that everything will be alright after the NSV or that things will continue as earlier. They could not explicitly state that their erection, ejaculation, and sexual pleasure will not be affected by the NSV.

It was found that the community members had no objection in listening to what the outreach workers were explaining. Nobody expressed concern about it being against their culture or tradition. After the discussions, many people appreciated the outreach workers for providing the needed information, and a classic response from some of the potential clients was, "this is exactly what I wanted to know."

After successful pretesting, the interventions were scaled up in nine districts of a province in India. About 600 outreach workers from public health facilities were trained in batches and they were encouraged to disseminate the information to potential clients in their villages through interpersonal communication. No financial incentives were given to these workers for this activity.

What Other Interventions Were Done?

Besides increasing demand, efforts were made to increase the availability of NSV services. 54 NSV surgeons were available in public health facilities in the intervention area. They were provided with supportive supervision and handholding by a few expert NSV surgeons of the project. Efforts were made to improve the quality of NSV services in these facilities.

What Were the Results?

It was found that the conversion for NSV acceptance was much higher when the outreach workers talked explicitly about erection, ejaculation, and sexual pleasure. Another realization was that if the spouse of a potential client is convinced, the chances of her husband accepting NSV are very high.

As a result of 2 years of these interventions, NSV acceptance in the nine project districts increased threefold from 1646 to 5009 men accepting NSV. During this period, the contribution of NSVs to total sterilizations increased from 2.4% to 9.1% in the project area. This data was obtained from the service statistics published by the department of health of the province.

Thus, if correct information is provided explicitly to potential clients, if their misconceptions are dispelled by providing scientific evidence, and if they have access to quality services, more of them are likely to utilize the services. Satisfied clients will disseminate the information through word of mouth and demand will increase.

Chapter 19

Human Resource Management

The department of human resource management, commonly known as HR, is responsible for providing manpower to various departments of the organization and coordinating their management. For example, in a hospital, the department of cardiothoracic surgery requires cardiac surgeons, senior and junior residents, nurses, a nurse supervisor and anesthetists. Technicians are required for performing tests such as angiography, ECG and TMT. A radiologist is required for interpreting the results of these tests and a perfusionist is required to assist in cardiac surgeries. The HR department coordinates the process of recruitment of the required manpower. In addition, it organizes the annual performance appraisal of all personnel of the organization, and coordinates the processes for granting raises, in salaries, or promotions. The department also coordinates the process for accepting resignations, terminations, or retirement. These functions are further explained subsequently.

227

Recruitment

The HR department coordinates the process of recruitment of manpower required by various departments of the organization. The recruitment process comprises the following steps:

- Securing sanctions and necessary approvals
- Advertising
- Receiving and screening applications
- Conducting telephone interviews
- Organizing personal interviews
- Organizing practical examinations/personality tests and selection
- Setting salaries
- Preparing offer letters/appointment letters
- Facilitating the coming on board of selected candidates
- Organizing induction training
- Placement

Ensuring sanctions and necessary approvals: Before initiating the process of recruitment, the HR department ensures that the position is sanctioned, it has been budgeted for in the annual budget of the organization, and has the approval of a competent authority.

Advertising: The HR department, after obtaining input from the concerned department, prepares the job specification for the position. Job specifications include the title of the position, qualifications, experience and skills required, key responsibilities, and any other requirements, such as the need to travel in rural areas (Figure 19.1).

The advertisement is posted on relevant Internet sites. It may appear as an advertisement in newspapers or professional journals. Some organizations give preference to internal candidates and circulate the information among concerned staff members before posting it on a website.

Job specifications

Title of the position:	**Clinical services executive**
Organization:	MS International, Address XYZ, website, contact email id
Department:	Clinical Services Department
Reports to:	Director Clinical Services

Background

MS International provides clinical family planning services in 24 outreach sites in rural and remote areas of a province in India.

Key Responsibilities

The key responsibility of the clinical services executive will be to assist the director of clinical services in managing documentation, such competency assessment report of clinical team members, internal quality assessment report of outreach teams, training reports, data of medical emergencies or incidents.

The clinical services executive will also visit each outreach site by turn and provide supportive supervision to the nursing staff working at the site. She will assess the quality of services, particularly infection prevention protocols and medical emergency preparedness in these camps. She will provide on the job support and training to nurses. She will prepare a brief report of her key observations, remedial actions taken, and recommendations.

Qualification

Bachelor of nursing from a prestigious institution

Experience

2–3 years' experience will be preferred. However, fresh graduates will also be considered if a suitable experienced candidate is not found.

Skills

1. Excellent documentation skills
2. Computer skills, particularly MS word and excel
3. Excellent interpersonal communication skills
4. Training skills

Other Requirements

Frequent travel in rural and remote areas is required. She may have to travel about 10 days a month.

Salary

Gross salary $10,000-12,000 per annum depending on qualification and experience, plus benefits

Last Date of Submission of CV along with Cover Letter: 25 August 2017

Figure 19.1   Example of job specifications.

Receiving and screening applications: In response to the posted advertisement, HR receives applications from interested candidates. An HR manager screens the applications to short-list the candidates that fulfill the minimum requirements in terms of qualification, number of years of relevant experience, computer skills, location, and so on. A matrix, as provided subsequently, can be helpful in screening the applications (Table 19.1).

Table 19.1 Example of a Matrix for Screening Job Applications

S. N.	Name of the Candidate	Qualification	Location	2 years' Experience	MS Word Skills	Excel Skills	Willingness to Travel	Salary Requirements Meeting Org. Norms	Remarks
1	AB	B.Sc. Nursing	Delhi	Y	Y	Y	Y	Y	Shortlisted
2	CD	M.Sc. Nursing	Patna	N	Y	N	N	N	X
3	EF	B.Sc. Nursing	Delhi	N	Y	Y	Y	Y	Shortlisted
4	GH	Registered Nurse	Mumbai	N	Y	N	Y	N	X

Telephonic interviews: An experienced HR manager conducts telephone interviews with the shortlisted candidates to check the information provided by the candidates and to further clarify the issues that were not included in the resume or application of the candidates. For example, if the job requires frequent travel to remote areas, the HR manager checks the willingness of the candidates for the same. If the job requires advanced Excel skills, the HR manager can clarify if the candidate can sort data or prepare pivot tables, and so on. It is also important to know the salary requirements of the candidates. Sometimes the salary requirement of a potential candidate is not asked at the beginning and candidates that are already getting a higher salary pass through the entire process of selection, which eventually turns out to be futile.

Personal interviews: In coordination with the head of the concerned departments, an HR manager organizes personal interviews with shortlisted candidates. A different time slot is allocated to different candidates to keep their waiting time to a minimum. In these interviews, the head of the concerned department takes the lead and examines the candidates for their knowledge on a subject and aptitude for the job. If there are many vacancies, a selection board comprised of three or more experts can be constituted.

Practical examination: If required, the head of the department organizes a practical test for the potential candidates to assess their skills. For example, to assess the training skills of a candidate, he may be asked to take a session with a staff member of the organization. To test computer skills, the candidate can be given an exercise to work on a computer.

Some positions may require a personality test. There are specialized agencies that conduct personality tests. These can also be conducted online.

The selection board or the head of the concerned department makes the final selection of the candidates.

Salary fixation: A senior HR manager negotiates the salary with the selected candidate. This is generally done within pre-fixed salary brackets. Organizations generally have fixed salary brackets for various cadres and positions, keeping in view the market trends. The tendency to hire candidates at the lowest possible salary should be resisted as it will eventually lead to a decline in the level of expertise in the organization.

Appointment letter: Some organizations first provide an offer letter to selected candidate indicating the salary, date of joining, and other terms and conditions. When the candidate accepts the offer, a formal appointment letter is issued. However, some organizations directly provide the appointment letter. A detailed job description is provided along with the appointment letter (Figure 19.2).

Orientation program: Upon their joining, the HR department organizes an orientation program for the new candidates. The program may be of one or more days depending on the nature of the job. Orientation includes an introduction to other staff members of the organization, different departments and their activities, and leave and travel-related rules. Then the line manager clarifies what exactly the candidate is expected to do and what his expectations are.

Placement: After the orientation, the candidates are placed in their actual place of work.

Performance appraisal

The HR department initiates and coordinates the process of annual performance appraisal for all staff members in the organization. During a specific time of the year, generally in January, each staff member is required to write a self-appraisal based on a prescribed format, in which they explain their achievements and reasons for shortfall, if any. The direct line manager reviews it and agrees or disagrees with the remarks of the staff member. Further, the line manager gives his opinion about the conduct and performance of the staff member and grades his performance as: excellent, good, satisfactory, or poor. The line

---

Job Description of a Nurse in Clinical Outreach

As a nurse of a clinical outreach team of MS International based at Luwasa, you will be reporting to the Team Leader and Surgeon. You will visit outreach camps along with other clinical team members and will be responsible for the following functions:

Client safety
- Ensure safety, privacy, and dignity of clients at every stage in the process of receiving services.

Clinical procedures
- Ensure readiness of Operation Theatre: its cleanliness, segregation of sterile and unsterile areas, organizing of instruments and other supplies, appropriate positioning of OT table and OT lights, availability of OT attire for the clinical team members.
- During the procedures, ensure availability of the required equipment, sterile supplies, disinfectants, and other materials required for the procedures.
- Manage infection prevention in accordance with organizational protocols.
- Assist the surgeon in conducting screening, pre-procedure assessment, per vaginal examination, administering anaesthesia, carrying out clinical procedures, elevating uterus when required by the surgeon.
- Ensure safe handling of laparoscopes and other equipment.
- Organize post-operative monitoring of the clients and providing them post-operative instructions.
- Organize post-operative follow-up of the clients.

Emergency preparedness
- Ensure availability of emergency medicines, equipment, and supplies.
- Manage emergencies, if any: provide   first aide and timely referral.

Documentation
- Maintain documents-record of surgeries, consumption of medicines and other supplies and other relevant registers.

Pre-camp preparations
Supervise pre-camp preparations like autoclaving, checking fitness of equipment, and adequacy of other supplies.

Figure 19.2   An example of job responsibilities of a nurse in clinical outreach.

manager's comments are reviewed by his supervisor, who is also required to agree or disagree with the comments of the line manager. The basic idea of a performance appraisal is to differentiate between good and poor performers. In many organizations, the purpose of a performance appraisal is defeated as almost all the staff members get a "good" rating. This is because many supervisors are not able to give definite comments about their subordinates because they fail to measure their performance based on defined criteria.

Increment and promotion

HR coordinates the process of setting the annual raises of the staff members, which is generally based on the grades achieved by them in their performance appraisal.

Resignation

When appointing a person, a notice period is defined, which either party is required to give while deciding a separation. The period is generally 1–3 months and is mentioned in the appointment letter. A staff member can submit his resignation giving notice as per the terms and conditions of his appointment. The authority that appointed him can only accept his resignation. The staff member is required to serve during the notice period and thereafter he is allowed to relinquish his charges and responsibilities. The HR department coordinates the process of separation of a staff member. The department ensures that the staff member surrenders the assets and documents of the organization and the computer password. The staff is asked to obtain a 'no dues certificate' from the relevant departments before relieving. HR also decides what payments the staff member is entitled to. For example, some organizations make payment in lieu of unused leave. Some organizations pay a gratuity to staff members who have served 5 years or more. HR prepares a full and final payment bill, and provides it to the finance department to release the payment. The HR department obtains formal feedback from the leaving staff member about the working conditions of the organization and grievances, if any. Staff suggestions are sought for improving working conditions or what could be done to retain staff. HR submits the feedback to the higher authority along with their recommendation.

In case a staff member wants to leave early without serving the required notice period, the leave earned by him can be adjusted against the notice period. The appointing authority may use its discretionary power to waive a part of his notice period. If the notice period is not waived by the competent authority and the staff member wants to be relieved early, he may have to pay the organization an amount equal to his salary for that period.

Memorandum

Date: 21 November 2017

From: XF, Operations Manager
To: CZ, Program Officer, District Zimawa
Subject: Performance

You were posted to district Zimawa on 1 October, 2016 with the primary objective of increasing demand for and utilization of IUCD services in the district. If you see the quarterly family planning statistics of the district, there is absolutely no improvement in IUCD utilization. In fact, there is some decline as shown below:

Quarter	IUCD acceptors
Quarter 4, 2016:	106
Quarter 1, 2017:	115
Quarter 2, 2017	82
Quarter 3, 2017	63

You were required to do mapping of all public and private health facilities of the district that provide IUCD services. You were required to assess the quality of services in these facilities. But, you have not yet shared these documents. You are once again reminded to submit the same by 1 December, 2017.

You are also advised to prepare a systematic plan for increasing awareness of the communities on IUCD and share it with me by 15 December, 2017.

Signature

Figure 19.3   Memorandum.

Retirement

Some organizations have a policy to retire the staff members upon attaining a certain age, which is generally 60–65 years. HR is required to keep track of the age of each staff member and issue a prior notice to the individual. Other activities are similar to resignation.

Termination

Termination of a staff member is one of the most challenging tasks in an organization and HR is expected to take a lead in the process. If a supervisor is not satisfied with the performance of his subordinate, and the latter is not willing to improve despite all possible efforts by the supervisor, the supervisor can seek the assistance of the HR department to initiate the process for terminating the staff member's services. To begin with, the staff member's performance is measured

---

Memorandum

Date: 18 December, 2017

From: Ms XF, Operations Manager
To: Mr CZ, Program Officer, District Zimawa

Subject: Show cause notice

The number of IUCD acceptors in your report of district Zimawafor Quarter III, 2017 was 63, whereas service statistics of the District Health Officer indicate the number of IUCD acceptors 28.

It seems you had inflated the figures to exaggerate your performance. You are hereby required to explain in writing the reasons for this lapse. Your reply should reach me by 21 December 2017. In case you fail to submit the reply or are not able to justify, administrative action will be initiated against you.

Signature

Figure 19.4   Show cause notice.

against defined standards. If his performance does not meet the requirements, a formal letter or memorandum is issued to him, indicating the gaps in his performance and an opportunity is given to improve within a specific period (Figure 19.3).

After 1 month, if there is no improvement, a warning letter is issued. After another month if there is no further improvement, a show cause notice is given, asking the staff member to explain why his performance is not up to the required level (Figure 19.4).

Upon getting a reply, the line manager of the staff member and HR department jointly decide whether the staff is justified or not. If they are not satisfied with the response, the department head and the HR head can jointly decide to go ahead with termination. A termination letter is prepared by HR and provided to the staff. The organization can decide to pay the salary in lieu of the notice period or allow him to work during the notice period, and then the staff member is allowed to leave.

Service Records

An important responsibility of the HR department is to maintain service records for each staff member. The service file contains the appointment letter offered to the individual, terms and conditions of the service, job responsibilities of the position, performance appraisal, raises, rewards earned, memorandum or punishments received by the individual, and time for retirement or separation.

Organizational Behavior

Since individuals and groups of people work in an organization, many interpersonal dynamics are in operation. Every individual is different in terms of his or her nature, motivation, behavior, habits, working style, ego, and many other factors. Accordingly, there are possibilities for differences of opinion and conflicts. The branch of management that deals with such dynamics in an organization is known as "organizational behavior." Many managers make a simple assumption that when staff members are employed and promptly paid their wages, they should work; they have to work. But it is not that simple. People need conducive environments to work optimally. The salary, benefits, and status that motivated an individual to join a job, cease to motivate him after some time. Efforts need to be made in the organization to keep the staff in high spirits and motivated.

Bibliography

Nancy Borkowski, *Organizational Behavior in Health Care*, Jones and Bartlett Publishers, 2nd edn., Sudbury, MA 2011.
Sharon B. Buchbinder et al., *Introduction to Health Care Management*, Jones and Bartlett Learning, 2nd edn., Burlington, MA 2012.

Chapter 20

Financial Management

The department of accounts and finance is responsible for the accounting of income and expenses of an organization and analyzing financial data. For obvious reasons, top management and the owners of organizations are especially interested in financial management.

Whenever a payment is received in an organization, an entry is made in the accounting books in chronological order of the receipt. The client who makes the payments gets the receipt, the counterfoil of which is retained by the organization. Similarly, when the organization makes a payment against a bill, the original bill is retained by the organization. Incomes and expenditure are booked against specific budget heads.

Finance department prepares financial statements to show an organization's financial health. The income–expenditure statement, also known as the profit and loss (P&L) statement, lists the revenues and expenses for a specific period, showing the organization's net profit or loss for that period. The department is also responsible for preparing the balance sheet that provides a snapshot of the company's assets and liabilities. Assets include land, buildings, equipment, other inventory, cash in hand, and money deposited in the bank. Liabilities include debts, taxes, and other payables. These accounts are prepared in accordance with the Companies Act and are required to be audited by a firm of chartered accountants within a prescribed time. Duly audited accounts are placed before the management board of the organization or shareholders within a prescribed time.

The finance department is also responsible for preparing the annual statement of accounts in accordance with income tax rules and regulations, for the purpose of income tax assessment. It also submits periodical returns to various direct and indirect tax authorities. Advance taxes and so on, must be deposited in the government account within prescribed time limits.

The finance department is invariably comprised of qualified managers to carry out an internal audit of the organization. The purpose of an internal audit is to keep the top management informed of compliance of financial guidelines and corrective actions on the previous audit report.

The system of accounting and finance of healthcare organizations with which managers of an organization must be familiar are explained in subsequent sections.

Income–Expenditure in Hospitals

In a hospital setting, income comes from user charges paid by clients for various services. Expenses include staff salaries; payments for medicines, equipment, linen, general stores, and other purchases; electricity bills; payments for services contracted out such as housekeeping, maintenance, security, linen and laundry, food and beverages, parking, and so on.

Analysis of Financial Date in a Hospital

Financial data is analyzed to reach conclusions and to make required decisions. For example, the financial performance of different departments can be compared to identify the departments that makes profit and those incurring losses. Efforts can be made to identify the underlying reasons for losses. Interventions can be made to revive the loss-incurring departments by inducting higher-level consultants, purchasing high-tech equipment or training staff in behavioral aspects. The management may also consider making an investment in marketing. In exceptional cases, decisions can be taken to close the department.

Similarly, the financial gain from various consultants can be analyzed, and the consultants who are not profitable for the hospital can be identified and decisions can be taken in this regard. The types of surgeries, procedures, or diagnostic tests that yield high returns can be identified. This information can be useful when plans are prepared for expansion of the hospital.

The previously mentioned analysis is possible only if relevant data is captured at the time of financial transaction. For example, if we want to compare the hospital's income from various consultants, the cashier will have to specify the name of the consultant and type of service against when a payment is received from a client.

Sharing Hospital Profit

Revenue from outpatient consultants should ideally be divided between the hospital and the consultants. But, some hospitals do not take their share and pass on the entire amount to the consultant concerned. This arrangement is based on the understanding that the hospital will earn its profit from the clients who get admitted or undergo diagnostic tests or surgeries.

Room or bed charges recovered from admitted clients go to the hospital account. However, when a consultant visits a client in his ward, visit charges are added to the client bill, which will be credited to the account of the consultant.

From the revenues recovered from a surgery, after deducting the direct expenses such as the cost of a stent, the remaining amount is shared between the hospital and surgeon. The other staff involved in a surgery, including the anesthetist and nurses, are generally on the payroll of the hospital and do not receive a share of this revenue.

Every expense incurred by a hospital, to the extent possible, is booked against a specific department. Common expenses, such as electricity, maintenance, housekeeping, or security are booked under "overheads" which is apportioned to all departments.

Financial Issues in Healthcare Organizations

Nongovernmental organizations (NGOs) or healthcare organizations generally are sustained by funds from donors. Donors generally sanction funds against an agreed upon budget submitted by the organization. Installments are generally released quarterly or annually. Major heads under which funds are allocated include

- Project staff salaries
- Project direct expenses—awareness generation, training, clinics, and so on.
- Consultant charges
- Project staff travel expenses for field level interventions
- Office staff travel expenses for monitoring and supervision
- International travel by international consultants or by national staff to attend meetings or conferences
- Training expenses for staff
- Workshops or conferences organized under the project
- Office expenses—of national office, provincial office, district offices—including rent, housekeeping, security, equipment, such as computers, office furniture, stationary, and other expenses.

- Overheads—of the national and international entities of the organization

Many healthcare organizations conduct awareness-generation activities for various sections of society. Some organizations conduct training for various groups of healthcare service providers. Some organizations provide direct services to communities and incur expenditure on medicines or family-planning commodities. All such expenses are included in the project budget.

Some NGOs work for the government and are reimbursed for services they provide to the community. This generally covers a part of the total expenses incurred by the organization.

The finance department of such healthcare organizations receives the bills and vouchers from the field staff. The accounts person determines the "head" under which the amount will be booked. The project manager approves the bill and payment is released to the staff concerned.

The finance department is expected to analyze the financial data. For example, if the organization provides services, the unit cost of each service can be determined. Trends of unit cost of a service over the years can be plotted on a graph and compared with the prevailing inflation rate to determine if there is a net change in the unit cost; to determine if the cost containment measures have been successful. Similarly, efficiency of various departments or services can be compared.

Chapter 21

Materials Management

In a hospital, after human resources, materials and medicines are the second largest consumer of its budget. The pharmacy is a major source of profit in private hospitals; accordingly, medicines and materials are of particular interest to management. The terms, materials management, logistics management, and supply chain management are often used interchangeably. The discipline of materials management aims to ensure the availability of the right materials (in terms of quantity and quality) at the right time, in the right place, and at a minimum cost. It involves planning, procurement, storage, and distribution of materials. Every item has to be accounted from the point of procurement until its consumption or disposal.

Classification of Materials

The varied types of materials utilized in a hospital include

- Medical supplies like medicines: Tablets, capsules, syrups, injections, inhalers, ointments, and eyedrops.
- Intravenous fluids: The amount of intravenous fluids used in specialized hospitals is so large that many hospitals have to maintain an exclusive store for them.

- Surgical supplies like surgical instruments; disposables like syringes, infusion sets; and dressing materials and plaster of Paris.
- Operation theater supplies like cardiac stents, eye lenses, plates and nails for fixing fractures.
- Laboratory items like glassware, reagents, and X-ray films.
- Linen like bed sheets, blankets, patient dresses, surgeon gowns, and surgical drapes.
- Equipment like cardiac monitors, urine flow meters, and X-ray machines.
- Furniture like patient beds, bedside lockers, and trolleys.
- Stationery like registers, files, laboratory requisition forms.
- Engineering items like spare parts for equipment, electrical fittings, and sanitation fittings.
- General and housekeeping items like dusters, brooms, tissue paper, soap, and detergent.

While procuring an item, it is important to determine whether it is consumable or not. This is important from the perspective of accounting since separate stock ledgers are maintained for consumable and nonconsumable items:

- *Consumables*: In a hospital, items such as medicines, X-ray films, or detergent are consumed regularly. Upon their consumption or sale, they are deducted from the stock ledger.
- *Nonconsumables*: Items such as surgical instruments, biomedical equipment, patient furniture, or oxygen tanks remain in use for several years. After such an item outlives its utility, it is subjected to condemnation procedures and then written off from the stock ledger.

  Items like bed sheets seem to be nonconsumable, but their turnover is so fast that some hospitals set an average life for bed sheets and automatically deduct them from the stock after the stipulated period.

Another important concern for a manager is knowing whether the item that is being procured will be charged to a patient or not.

■ *Items chargeable to patients*: Items, such as medicines, intravenous fluids, or medical gases are administered to patients and their cost is directly recovered from patients.
■ *Items not chargeable to patients*: Certain items like cleaning materials or engineering spare parts are used in the hospital, but their cost is not directly charged to individual patients. Their expenses are included in the overhead of the hospital, which is eventually passed on to the patients on a pro rata basis.

Organization of Materials Management Department

The materials management department in a hospital is generally headed by a mid-level manager, and sometimes by a top-level manager. The department is comprised of three main sections: procurement section, central store, and pharmacy. Each section is headed by an assistant manager. The central store can have several substores, such as medical stores, surgical stores, operating room store, inpatient store, linen store, stationery store, engineering/maintenance store, and general stores. Each substore is headed by a store in-charge or a senior pharmacist (Figure 21.1).

Location of Stores

The central store can be located in a nonprime area of the hospital. However, the pharmacy should be located in a prominent location in the outpatient clinics area. In the case of space constraint in the outpatient clinic area, a small pharmacy outlet with an effective back-end support from a

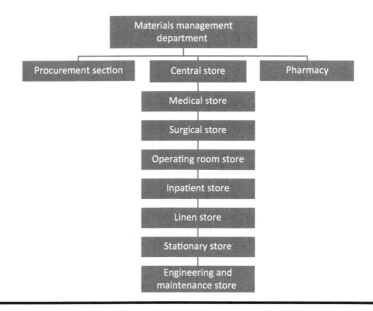

Figure 21.1   Organization of materials management department.

warehouse can serve the purpose. The operating room store should be located in the operation theater complex. Other substores like the linen store and stationery store can be placed anywhere in nonprime areas of the hospital. The linen store can have a tailor shop for preparing drapes for the operating rooms and repairing surgical attire or patient dresses. The engineering or maintenance store should be located close to the engineering workshop or garage. They are generally placed in basements.

Functions of Materials Management Department

The materials management department broadly performs three functions:

- Procurement
- Inventory management
- Supply, issue or disposal

Procurement

The process of purchasing involves the following activities:

1. Planning and budgeting
2. Demand forecasting
3. Purchase approval
4. Selection of brands and vendors
5. Purchase orders
6. Receipt of goods
7. Entering the goods into a stock ledger
8. Payment to vendor

Planning and Budgeting

The top management of an organization generally decides the budget for purchasing materials in each financial year. Funds are allocated separately for nonconsumable and consumable items and the two budget heads are generally not interchangeable.

For the medicines and surgical consumables that are charged to patients, the hospital makes a one-time investment. The cost of these materials is recovered from the patients and thereafter the fund keeps rolling. In fact, with the addition of profit, the inventory can keep growing.

For the purchase of major equipment, the heads of departments generally prepare a case justifying their demand. Equipment like a CT scan, MRI, or gamma knife are expensive and it takes several years to recover their cost. The top management or management board, keeping in view the estimated expenses and projected financial returns, draws up a long-term plan for purchasing expensive equipment.

There is a long list of medicines and materials available in the market, and new products keep adding to this list. Consultants and other hospital staff keep demanding new products. As a result, the hospital inventory keeps growing. It is important, though challenging, for a manager to resist such pressure and keep the inventory limited; otherwise the stores would become chaotic. Public hospitals can adopt a list of essential medicines, and limit their inventory to the defined list. Many such lists, including one prepared by the WHO, are available. Consultants should be persuaded to prescribe medicines from the list to the extent possible. There can be exceptional situations when a required medicine is not included in the list and the patient concerned is advised to purchase them from the market. On the other hand, private hospitals earn major profits from the pharmacy, so they like to stock everything that can be sold readily. The materials manager and heads of the clinical departments can reach an understanding on the list of medicines to be kept in the hospital store. This is known as the hospital formulary. The materials management department should try to ensure the availability of every item of the hospital formulary in their stock and the consultants should try to restrict their prescriptions to the formulary.

Demand forecasting

Projections for consumable items are generally made on the basis of the previous year's consumption. In case there are significant variations in the monthly consumption of an item, its consumption during the same month in the previous year can be taken as a benchmark. Increasing or decreasing trends, if any, in the consumption of an item can also be taken into consideration while making the projections. The storekeeper or service providers often have a fair idea of the requirements of various items. For example, the manager of linen and laundry services is likely to know the requirement of bed sheets; the engineer may have a better idea of the requirement of engineering spare parts.

If an item is consumed in large quantities, its annual requirement can be broken down into monthly or weekly requirements, accordingly, purchase orders can be placed. In big cities, most of the items are readily available in the market and, many busy pharmacies get their replenishments on a daily basis. However, in rural and far-flung areas, the availability of certain goods may not be certain, and careful planning would be required to prevent stock-out situations.

Purchase Approval

Mere allocation of funds for certain items in the budget does not authorize a procurement officer to make purchases of those items. The approval of a competent authority is needed every time before a purchase is made. In every organization, specific officers are entrusted with certain financial powers to make purchases of specific categories of items and only they can approve the purchases of those goods. A department submits its requisition to the procurement officer, who seeks the approval of the competent authority before initiating the purchase procedures.

Selection of Brands and Vendors

Product information, such as available brands, their specifications and cost, and the authorized dealers, is mostly available on the Internet. If required, the staff concerned can carry out market surveys to identify the dealers who offer the products at competitive prices. Vendor engagement is a dynamic process, and new vendors should be inducted periodically.

To make purchase decisions, in many organizations, a purchase committee comprised of three or more officers is constituted. An officer from the department using the supplies, one from the materials management department, and one from finance make an ideal combination for the committee. After obtaining approval for the purchase of the required goods, the purchase officer arranges to obtain quotations from at least three vendors. A comparative statement is prepared and presented before the purchase committee (Figure 21.2).

The committee generally selects the lowest priced goods. And the committee also approved the vendors from whom the goods will be purchased. However, the committees are generally empowered to approve the purchase of an item at a higher

Comparative Statement

S.N.	Item	Quantity	Quotations		
			Sun Brothers Pharmaceuticals	YM Medicos	Messrs Z
1	Amoxicillin suspension (125 mg/5 ml), bottle of 60 ml.	One box of 100 bottles	Company A, brand name M $2000	Company B, brand name N $2200.50	Company C, brand name M $2100
2	Paracetamol syrup (125 mg/5 ml), bottle of 60 ml.	One box of 100 bottles	Company D, brand name O $1000	Company D, brand name O $1200	Company D, brand name O $1200
3	Ceftazidime injection 500 mg.	One packet of 10 ampules	Company E, brand name P $78	Company E, brand name P $78	Company F, brand name R $80
4	Cefadroxil tablet 500 mg.	One box of 100 tablets	Company E, brand name Q $102	Company E, brand name Q $105	Company G, brand name S $28
5	Artesunate injection 60 mg.	One packet of 4 ampules	Company H, brand name T $125	Company H, brand name T $126	Company H, brand name T $128

Recommendation of the Purchase Committee

Date: 27 April 2017

The purchase committee, having examined the quotations received from the three vendors mentioned above recommends to purchase amoxicillin suspension, paracetamol syrup, and artesunate injection from Sun Brothers Pharmaceuticals for their lowest prices.

However, for cefadroxil tablet, although the quotation of Messrs Z is lowest, the committee recommends to purchase it from Sun Brothers Pharmaceuticals since their product is from a reputed manufacturer.

Signature	Signature	Signature
Presiding Office	Member 1	Member 2

Figure 21.2   An example of a comparative statement.

price based on its merits. In such a situation, the committee is required to explain in writing the reason for their decision.

In many situations, a system of three quotations does not serve the desired purpose. For example, if a person wants to purchase an item at a higher cost, it may not be difficult for him to obtain quotations with even higher quotes. Therefore, many organizations have discontinued this practice. In that case, the purchase committee conducts a market survey; negotiates with the vendors, and makes the purchases at the best price. This requires trust in the officers.

To make purchase of large quantities of goods or expensive equipment, a better option is to float tenders and invite bids. An advertisement is posted in popular newspapers or on the Internet providing information to a wider range of vendors. The vendors, who are interested in supplying the items, submit their quotations in a prescribed format in a sealed cover within a fixed deadline. The purchase committee members assemble on a predetermined day and time and open the tenders. A comparative statement is prepared and purchase decisions are made.

Purchase Order

Once the purchase committee approves the rate at which the goods can be purchased and the vendor from whom goods can be purchased, the procurement section prepares a purchase order and submits it to the selected vendor. The purchase order is addressed to a particular vendor and provides detailed information about the goods that are to be purchased, their brand names, specifications, quantity, unit cost, taxes, and the total cost. The timeline for the delivery of goods is specified. Information is also provided on when the payment will be made and the mode of payment. In the case of equipment or expensive items, particular care is taken to write detailed specifications. Subject experts' help should be obtained for writing the specifications. A purchase order is an important document, particularly in the case of any discrepancy in supply or dispute with the vendor; it can be helpful in clarifying doubts and assigning responsibility (Figure 21.3).

Receipt of Goods

After receiving the purchase order, the vendor supplies the goods along with two copies of the invoice. Upon receipt of the

Rose Well Hospital
Rouse Avenue, Connaught Place, New Delhi 110007
www.rosewellhospital.org
purchaseofficer@rosewell.org; +91-22-22345688

28 April 2017

Sun Pharma Brothers
R-77, Red Cross Road, Santa Cruz,
Mumbai East, Maharashtra, India

Subject: Purchase order No. 71/ July 2017
Reference: Your quotation no. 123 dated 20 July 2017

Dear Sir/ Madam
You are requested to supply the following medicines:

S.N.	Brand name, Chemical, Manufacturer	Unit	Unit cost $	Quantity	Total cost $
1	Brand M, Amoxicillin suspension (125 mg/5 ml), bottle of 60 ml, Company A	One box of 100 bottles	2000	1 box	2000
2	Band O, Paracetamol syrup (125 mg/5 ml), bottle of 60 ml, Company D.	One box of 100 bottles	1000	1 box	1000
3	Brand P, Ceftazidime injection 500 mg, Company E.	One packet of 10 ampules	78	10 packets	780
4	Brand Q, Cefadroxil tablet 500 mg, Company E.	One box of 100 tablets	102	1 box	102
5	Brand T, Artesunate injection 60 mg, Company H.	One packet of 4 ampules	125	10 packets	1250
				Total	5132

You are requested to deliver the goods within 7 days of the receipt of this purchase order in the main store of the hospital at the above address along with the invoice.

The payment will be released through money transfer in your bank account within 15 days of receipt of the goods and advance receipt.

Signature
Procurement Officer

Figure 21.3   An example of a purchase order.

goods, it is the responsibility of the store in charge to inspect each item physically and tally them with the invoice. In the case of equipment, expensive items, or a large consignment, the inspection should be done by the purchase committee. The committee can also involve a subject expert to inspect technical equipment. Upon the satisfactory receipt of the goods, the store in charge certifies on a copy of the invoice that the goods have been received in the right quantity and quality and returns it to the supplier. He retains the second copy of the invoice.

Just-in-time concept: For expensive items, arrangements can be made with the vendors to supply them when they are actually needed, so the hospital does not have to maintain a stock of such items. This is known as the "just-in-time concept." The operating room stores mostly operate on this concept. The surgeons and nurses concerned provide a list of items required for the next day's surgeries. The store in charge compiles requirements from all concerned and forwards them to a vendor, who confirms their availability and supplies the items on the next day's morning, before the surgeries start. The prices of major goods are generally predecided. Vendors with a high reliability are engaged for such arrangements since any delay in supply may result in the cancellation of surgeries, which can cost a hospital dearly. Thus, the hospital is saved from investing in maintaining an inventory and the space it would occupy.

Bar-code System: Hospitals can opt for a bar code system. At the time of receiving the goods in the store, a specific bar code is generated by the computer for each item. The bar code sticker is fixed on each item. It helps in their identification and billing.

Entering the Goods into a Stock Ledger

After receiving the goods, entry is made for each item in the stock ledger. Corporate hospitals mostly maintain their stock ledgers on computers.

Payment to the Vendor

After having received the goods and ensuring entry of each item in the stock ledger, the procurement officer verifies the bills received from the vendor and forwards them to the finance department to release payments.

There are different modes for making payments to vendors. When payments are made to the vendor after receiving the goods, the procedure is known as "purchase on credit." Certain items may not be available on credit and the vendor may demand the payment at the time of delivery of the goods. For certain products, the vendor may demand an advance payment (part or full) along with the purchase order. In such situations, the procurement officer, in addition to obtaining approval for the purchase also seeks approval for making advance payments to the vendor.

Inventory Management

The term "inventory" refers to the goods available in a store or facility. Management of goods in a store or facility is known as inventory management.

Distribution of Goods to Substores

For better control, all purchases in a hospital should be made centrally and all good received in the central store. From the central store, they are further distributed to other substores or user departments. However, some hospitals make exceptions for the outpatient clinic pharmacy and operating room store to function independently. When goods are transferred from one store to another, the storekeeper of the first store prepares an issue voucher in duplicate. Upon receipt of the goods, the storekeeper of the receiving store signs a copy of the voucher, returns it to the issuing storekeeper, and retains the other copy with him. Issue vouchers can be helpful in tracking the movement of goods within the organization. After receiving the goods, the store keeper of the substore ensures their entry in his stock ledger. In computerized systems, these entries are made automatically when the goods are transferred from the main store ledger.

There are disadvantages to a large inventory. It occupies a large space and ties up hospital funds. Retrieving an item from a large store can be challenging. Also, medicines have a limited shelf life. Goods must be protected from pilferage, rodents, and infestations. The proper temperature and humidity is to be maintained in medicine stores. Thus, there is a cost to maintaining inventory, which is known as the "carrying cost."

Stacking of Medicines in a Store

The retail pharmacy outlets generally stack medicines on their shelves according to the names of the manufacturing companies. For example, all medicines from the Merck Company are stacked on one shelf, and all medicines of GlaxoSmithKline are kept on another. This arrangement makes it convenient for the storekeeper to place a purchase order with the vendor of a company. By looking at a particular shelf, he can identify all requirements from that company.

A scientific and better method of stacking the medicines in a store is according to their category, therapeutic action, or chemical. For example, all antibiotics, such as amoxicillin, azithromycin, ciprofloxacin, cephalexin, tetracycline, and so on, can be kept in one place. And all analgesics, such as diclofenac, ibuprofen, paracetamol, and so on, can be kept on one side. They can be further classified according to their chemical or salt. For example, all preparations of amoxicillin from various manufacturers can be stacked together. The advantage of this system is that a new pharmacist can understand the system quickly. Secondly, if a medicine from a particular company is not available, its alternative from another company can be identified easily, since it would be stacked close by. However, in a computerized system, there can be other ways of finding an alternative for a medicine.

Inventory Control

There can be several thousand items in a hospital store, and it is virtually impossible for a manager to monitor every item. The only option for a manager is to prioritize the items that need close monitoring and delegate subordinates to monitor the other items. Medicines and other hospital goods can be prioritized based on

1. Their value in saving lives: VED analysis
2. Their cost implications: ABC analysis

VED analysis: VED analysis is a method for classifying hospital inventory into three categories according to its value in saving lives:

V: Vital
E: Essential
D: Desirable

Vital items are those that can save a life; their nonavailability may result in death; for example, emergency medicines (given in Table 21.1) are "vital." In specialized hospitals, equipment such as a defibrillator, ventilators, or suction/vacuum can be considered vital. Diarrhea and acute respiratory infections are the two most common causes of death in children in developing countries. In community-based health facilities, supplies of oral rehydration salt, to manage diarrhea, and pediatric antibiotic preparations, to manage acute respiratory infections, can be considered vital. The manager of a healthcare facility dealing with materials should give top priority to the availability of vital medicines and equipment.

Essential medicines are required for treating commonly prevalent diseases or conditions. Their non-availability may not immediately lead to a death. However, they are essential to running a facility. For example, in the areas where malaria, tuberculosis, or kala-azar are prevalent, medicines used in their

Table 21.1   List of Medicines and Supplies in a Primary Health Center

S.N.	Name of Item	S.N.	Name of Item
	Analgesics		**Steroids**
1	Paracetamol tablet 500 mg	27	Prednisolone tablet 5 mg
2	Paracetamol syrup (125 mg/5 ml) 60 ml	28	Prednisolone syrup 120 ml, 5 mg/ml
3	Ibuprofen tablet 400 mg		**Antihelmenthic**
4	Ibuprofen syrup (100 mg/5 ml) 120 ml	30	Albendazole 400 mg
5	Diclofenac + paracetamol tablet	31	Albendazole syrup 10 ml, 100 mg/5 ml
6	Diclofenac injection (25 mg/ml) 3 ml		**Eye/Eardrops**
	Antibiotics	33	Ciprofloxacin eye/eardrop 7.5 ml
8	Amoxicillin capsule 250 mg		**Dressing Materials**
9	Amoxicillin chewable tablet 250 mg	35	Cotton roll- 500 gm
10	Amoxicillin susp. (250 mg/5 ml) 100 ml	36	Gauze roll
11	Azithromycin tablet 500 mg	37	Bandage 4 inch, packet of 12
12	Ciprofloxacin tablet 500 mg	38	Betadine solution 100 ml
13	Ceftazidime injection 500 mg		**Family Planning Commodities**
14	Norfloxacin tablet 400 mg	39	Condoms
	Antidiarrhea, antiprotozoa	40	Oral contraceptive pills, strip of 28 pills
16	Oral rehydration salt		**Others**

(Continued)

Table 21.1 (Continued)   List of Medicines and Supplies in a Primary Health Center

S.N.	Name of Item	S.N.	Name of Item
17	Metranidazole 500 mg	41	Tetanus Toxoid Injection
	Antimalaria	42	Syringe 5 ml
19	Chloroquine tablet 500 mg	43	Iron 300 mg + folic acid 5 mg tablets
20	Artemisinin + lumefantrine tablet		**Emergency Medicines**
21	Artesunate injection 60 mg	44–51	Inj. adrenaline; Inj. hydrocortisone; Inj. chlorpheniramine maleate; Inj. atropine; tablet isosorbide mononitrate; Inj. ringer lactate; syringes and infusion sets.
	Bronchodilators		
23	Salbutamol inhaler 0.5 mg/ml		
24	Terbutaline tablet 5 mg		
25	Terbutaline syrup (2.5 mg/5ml), bottle of 60 ml.		

treatment can be considered "essential." In a conflict-affected area, dressing materials may be essential. In a tertiary-care hospital, a CT scan or MRI may be essential equipment, while in a secondary-level hospital, an X-ray machine is, and in a primary health center, a microscope may be essential equipment.

Vitamins and mineral preparations are mostly "desirable." Their nonavailability is not likely to pose any risk to the life of clients.

The manager should keep a close watch over vital medicines and equipment. After having been assured of their availability, depending on the situation, he may monitor the essential items or delegate their responsibility to a subordinate.

ABC analysis: This involves classifying the medicines according to their monetary value. It should be noted that the total purchase amount of an item is different from its unit cost. The total purchase amount of an item is derived by multiplying the unit cost by the number of units purchased. ABC analysis is based on total purchase amount for items and not on their unit cost. For example, a bottle of intravenous fluid is not very expensive, but intravenous fluids are utilized in large quantities in secondary- and tertiary-level hospitals resulting in high expenses.

To carry out an ABC analysis, all medicines in the inventory are listed (Table 21.1).

The unit cost of each medicine and their quantity are listed out. The amount of the purchase of each item is calculated by multiplying unit cost by quantity (see column 6 in Table 21.2).

Thereafter, these items are rearranged in descending order of the amount of their purchase (see column 7 in Table 21.3).

Another column for the cumulative amount is added. The second cell in this column gives the total amount for the first and second items. The third cell gives the total amount for the first, second, and third items, and so on (Table 21.3).

Table 21.2 shows that an inventory of 51 medicines costs a total amount of $106,600. Of the total amount, 70% of inventory amounts to $74,620. In the last column, you can see that out of a total of 51 medicines, only 7 medicines cost a little more than this amount. In other words 14% of the items cost about 70% of the inventory. It has been found that commonly 10–20% of items of an inventory cost 70–80% of the total amount. In other words, a few items account for a major chunk of inventory costs. It would always be convenient for a manager to keep a close watch over a few items. They are considered category "A" items. The manager can conduct random checks on some of these items to verify whether purchase procedures were followed diligently during their purchase, whether the costs at which they were purchased were

Table 21.2   List of Medicines with Amount

S.N.	Item	Accounting Unit	Unit Cost in $	Quantity Purchased	Amount of Purchase $
1	Paracetamol tablet 500 mg	Tab	0.04	10,000	400
2	Paracetamol syrup 60 ml, 125 mg/5 ml	Bot	10	1,000	10,000
3	Ibuprofen tablet 400 mg	Tab	0.25	5,000	1,250
4	Ibuprofen syrup 120 ml, 100 mg/5 ml	Bot	12.5	500	6,250
5	Diclofenac + Paracetamol tablet	Tab	0.4	5,000	2,000
6	Diclofenac injection 3 ml, 25 mg/ml	Ampule	1	1,000	1,000
8	Amoxicillin capsule 250 mg	Cap	0.4	5,000	2,000
9	Amoxicillin chewable tablet 250 mg	Tab	0.6	5,000	3,000
10	Amoxicillin susp. 100 ml, 250 mg/5 ml	Bot	31	1,000	31,000
11	Azithromycin tablet 500 mg	Tab	1.25	2,000	2,500
12	Ciprofloxacin tablet 500 mg	Tab	0.5	3,000	1,500
13	Ceftazidime injection 500 mg	Ampule	4.1	1,000	4,100
14	Norfloxacin 400 mg	Tab	0.3	1,000	300
16	Oral rehydration salt	Sachet	0.75	5,000	3,750
17	Metranidazole tablet 500 mg	Tab	1	500	500
19	Chloroquine tablet 500 mg	Tab	0.4	2,000	800
20	Artemisinin + lumefantrine tablet	Tab	0.9	1000	900

(*Continued*)

Table 21.2 (Continued)   List of Medicines with Amount

S.N.	Item	Accounting Unit	Unit Cost in $	Quantity Purchased	Amount of Purchase $
21	Artesunate injection 60 mg	Ampule	20	500	10,000
23	Salbutamol inhaler 0.5 mg/ml	Bot	25	100	2,500
24	Terbutaline tablet 5 mg	Tab	0.25	500	125
25	Terbutaline syrup 2.5 mg/5 ml	Bot	14	100	1,400
27	Prednisolone tablet 5 mg	Tab	0.4	500	200
28	Prednisolone syrup 120 ml, 5 mg/ml	Bot	10	100	1,000
30	Albendazome 400 mg	Tab	0.6	100	60
31	Albendazole syrup 10 ml, 100 mg/5ml	Bot	15	100	1,500
33	Ciprofloxacin eye/eardrop 7.5 ml	Vial	5.5	200	1,100
35	Cotton roll- 500 gm	Packet	10	100	1,000
36	Gauze roll	Roll	15	50	750
37	Bandage 4 inch, 12 number	Packet	1.5	500	750
38	Betadine solution 100 ml	Bottle	7.5	20	150
39	Condom	Piece	1	10,000	10,000
40	Oral contraceptive pills, 28 pills pack	Pack	6	500	3,000
41	Tetanus toxoid injection	Ampule	4	100	400
42	Syringe 5 ml	Piece	0.4	1,000	400
43	Iron 300 mg + folic acid 5 mg tablets	Tab	0.1	10,000	1,000
44-51	Emergency medicines	Amp/Bot	15	1	15
				Total	**106,600**

Table 21.3 Cumulative Amount Arranged in Ascending Order

S.N.	Item	Accounting Unit	Unit Cost $	Quantity	Amount $	Cumulative Amount $	% of Total Amount
10	Amoxicillin susp. 100 ml, 250 mg/5 ml	Bot	31	1,000	31000	31,000	70%
2	Paracetamol syrup 60 ml, 125 mg/5 ml	Bot	10	1,000	10000	41,000	
21	Artesunate injection 60 mg	Ampule	20	500	10000	51,000	
39	Condom	Piece	1	10,000	10000	61,000	
4	Ibuprofen syrup 120 ml, 100 mg/5 ml	Bot	12.5	500	6250	67,250	
13	Ceftazidime injection 500 mg	Ampule	4.1	1,000	4100	71,350	
16	Oral rehydration salt	Sachet	0.75	5,000	3750	75,100	
9	Amoxicillin chewable tablet 250 mg	Tab	0.6	5,000	3000	78,100	20%
40	Oral contraceptive pills, 28 pills pack	Pack	6	500	3000	81,100	
11	Azithromycin tablet 500 mg	Tab	1.25	2,000	2500	83,600	
23	Salbutamol inhaler 0.5 mg/ml	Bot	25	100	2500	86,100	
5	Diclofenac + paracetamol tablet	Tab	0.4	5,000	2000	88,100	
8	Amoxicillin capsule 250 mg	Cap	0.4	5,000	2000	90,100	
12	Ciprofloxacin tablet 500 mg	Tab	0.5	3,000	1500	91,600	

(Continued)

Table 21.3 (Continued) Cumulative Amount Arranged in Ascending Order

S.N.	Item	Accounting Unit	Unit Cost $	Quantity	Amount $	Cumulative Amount $	% of Total Amount
31	Albendazole syrup 10 ml, 100 mg/5 ml	Bot	15	100	1500	93,100	
25	Terbutaline syrup 2.5 mg/5 ml	Bot	14	100	1400	94,500	
3	Ibuprofen tablet 400 mg	Tab	0.25	5,000	1250	95,750	10%
33	Ciprofloxacin eye/eardrop 7.5 ml	Vial	5.5	200	1100	96,850	
6	Diclofenac injection 3 ml, 25 mg/ml	Ampule	1	1,000	1000	97,850	
28	Prednisolone syrup 120 ml, 5 mg/ml	Bot	10	100	1000	98,850	
35	Cotton roll- 500 gm	Packet	10	100	1000	99,850	
43	Iron 300 mg + folic acid 5 mg tablets	Tab	0.1	10,000	1000	100,850	
20	Artemisinin + lumefantrine tablet	Tab	0.9	1,000	900	101,750	
19	Chloroquine tablet 500 mg	Tab	0.4	2,000	800	102,550	
36	Gauze roll	Roll	15	50	750	103,300	
37	Bandage 4 inch, 12 number	Packet	1.5	500	750	104,050	
17	Metranidazole tablet 500 mg	Tab	1	500	500	104,550	

(Continued)

Table 21.3 (Continued)   Cumulative Amount Arranged in Ascending Order

S.N.	Item	Accounting Unit	Unit Cost $	Quantity	Amount $	Cumulative Amount $	% of Total Amount
1	Paracetamol tablet 500 mg	Tab	0.04	10,000	400	104,950	
41	Tetanus toxoid injection	Ampule	4	100	400	105,350	
42	Syringe 5 ml	Piece	0.4	1,000	400	105,750	
14	Norfloxacin 400 mg	Tab	0.3	1,000	300	106,050	
27	Prednisolone tablet 5 mg	Tab	0.4	500	200	106,250	
38	Betadine solution 100 ml	Bottle	7.5	20	150	106,400	
24	Terbutaline tablet 5 mg	Tab	0	500	125	106,525	
30	Albendazome 400 mg	Tab	0.6	100	60	106,585	
44–51	Emergency medicines	Amp/Bot	15	1	15	106,600	

appropriate, and whether the items were of good quality. He may also check if any category "A" item is shelved in the store for a long period and blocking money.

Items that cost the next 20% of inventory are considered "B" category, and the rest of that items that cost only 10% of inventory are labeled as "C" category. The manager may consider delegating responsibility of C or even B category items to his subordinates.

Expensive items: A manager may also track some of the expensive items (items with a high unit price) since they have higher chances of getting stolen.

First in-First out

A system should be set up in such a way that the items purchased early are sold off or issued first. When new stock of an item is purchased, it should be stacked behind the existing items.

Reorder Level

To prevent stock-out situations, before an item gets exhausted, the procurement process has to begin at an appropriate stage. The level of stock of an item at which a new purchase orders is placed is known as its "reorder level." The time taken by the organization to prepare a purchase order and to place it with a vendor is known as internal lead time. External lead time is the time taken by the vendor to supply the goods after receiving the purchase order. Reorder level of an item depends on the consumption of the item during the total lead period (internal + external). For example, if total lead time for procuring amoxicillin suspension is one month and in a month an average of 80 bottles of the medicine are consumed, then the procurement process has to start when at least 80 bottles are available in the stock. Keeping in mind the fact that sometimes there can be a fast consumption of a medicine, say during an epidemic, to be on a safer side, a buffer stock may be added. For example, in case of amoxicillin suspension, the procurement process may preferably start when its stock level reaches to 100–120 bottles. The reorder level of every item will vary depending on its consumption pattern. It is the responsibility of the store in charge to define the reorder level of very item in his store. Inventory modules can be programmed to raise an alert when the reorder level of an item is reached.

Similarly, it would be useful to define the maximum stock that would be maintained in a store. For example, a store manager may decide to stock supplies for a maximum period of 3 months. That means, in the above example, a maximum stock of 240 amoxicillin suspension bottles can be kept in the store. After one and a half months of replenishment when the stock level of the medicine drops to about 120 bottles, the procurement process may have to be started. A purchase order will be made for about 120 bottles so that the stock of amoxicillin does not exceed the limit of 240 bottles.

Sale, Issue, and Disposal of Goods

The outpatient pharmacy sells medicines and other medical goods upon cash payment to patients. However, in the case of inpatients, the amount is generally debited to their account. They can make payments periodically or at the time of their discharge.

When the goods are issued to various hospital departments for their use, the hospital bears the cost and a separate account is maintained for such expenses.

Condemnation Procedure

When equipment or a nonconsumable item breaks down, becomes unserviceable, or its repair is not cost-effective, it can be subjected to condemnation procedures and written off. The management of the organization constitutes a condemnation committee comprised of three or more officers. User departments prepare a list of items they want to write off indicating the

1. Name of each item
2. Quantity
3. Date of purchase
4. Unit cost and total cost of each item

The condemnation committee assembles on a predetermined day, examines each item, and scrutinizes their documents. If satisfied, the committee gives approval for their condemnation. They also recommend how each item will be disposed of: by selling it to a scrap dealer, by burning or burying it. Linen can be used for dusting or cleaning. Items that are recommended for sale are sold off, and the amount is deposited with the hospital treasury. Condemned items are written off from the stock ledger. The approval of the condemnation committee should be kept as authorization for writing of goods from the stock ledger.

In busy hospitals, there is a frequent need to write off items, such as bed sheets, blankets, buckets, mugs, utensils, dishes, and in some hospitals, the condemnation committee assembles every month.

Accounting of Goods

The organization maintains an accounting of each item from the point of its purchase until it is sold off to a patient, utilized in the hospital, or condemned and disposed of. Any item for which the organization has made a payment must be entered into the stock ledger of the store. From the central store, the items get transferred to other substores. Accordingly, transfers are made in the stock ledgers of the concerned stores. The pharmacy or inpatient substore sells the consumable items to patients. For example, patients are charged for oxygen on the basis of the hourly consumption of the gas. Similarly, they are charged for equipment, such as a ventilator or monitor as per usage. Some items, such as cleaning materials are issued to various hospital departments for their consumption, and the hospital bears their cost. These expenses are included in the overhead. The total overhead of the hospital is distributed among all patients.

Nonconsumable items depreciate every year. For example, a computer is expected to last 5 years. Every year, its value depreciates by 20%, so that after 5 years, its value is zero. Thereafter, it can be condemned and disposed of. Depreciation is adjusted in the annual accounts.

Role of a Manager

The most important role of a manager in the materials management department is to ensure the availability of required medicines and supplies in every service unit of the organization. There should never be a stock-out situation for any item at any point in time, particularly for the vital items. The manager should have a fair idea of the requirements for vital items, items that have a high purchase value, and expensive items. He should ensure that purchases are made at the most competitive prices and that they are of the required specification and quality.

The manager should make every possible effort to keep the inventory limited. He should be careful to avoid purchasing items that are not likely to be sold. In case some nonmoving items are stuck in the stores, he should make arrangements to dispose of them and clear the space.

The manager should monitor patients' satisfaction with pharmacy services. He should ensure that patients are not made to wait for long at the pharmacy and that they are provided with complete information about the medicines. The manager should also see to it that the user departments are satisfied with the central store.

The manager should organize stock-taking in the store, whereby each item of the inventory is physically verified and tallied with the stock ledger at least once a year.

The manager should measure the income from the pharmacy. He should be aware of the items that provide maximum profit. He should get monthly income–expenditure statements prepared.

Index